Writer's Companion

Support and Practice for Writing

Grade 3

Copyright © by Harcourt, Inc.

All rights reserved. No part of this publication may be reproduced or transmitted in any form or by any means, electronic or mechanical, including photocopy, recording, or any information storage and retrieval system, without permission in writing from the publisher.

Requests for permission to make copies of any part of the work should be addressed to School Permissions and Copyrights, Harcourt, Inc., 6277 Sea Harbor Drive, Orlando, Florida 32887-6777. Fax: 407-345-2418.

HARCOURT and the Harcourt Logo are trademarks of Harcourt, Inc., registered in the United States of America and/or other jurisdictions.

Printed in the United States of America

ISBN 0-15-349063-2

3 4 5 6 7 8 9 10 073 15 14 13 12 11 10 09 08 07 06

If you have received these materials as examination copies free of charge, Harcourt School Publishers retains title to the materials and they may not be resold. Resale of examination copies is strictly prohibited and is illegal.

Possession of this publication in print format does not entitle users to convert this publication, or any portion of it, into electronic format.

Contents

Introduction 4

UNIT 1
WRITER'S CRAFT: VOICE

LESSON 1 Sensory Details 8
Literature Model Officer Buckle and Gloria
Student Model Descriptive Paragraph

LESSON 2 Expressing Your Viewpoint 14
Literature Model Pepita Talks Twice
Student Model Journal/Diary Entry

LESSON 3 Expressing Feelings 20
Literature Model Nate the Great, San Francisco Detective
Student Model Personal Narrative

Test Prep **LESSON 4 Review/Extended Written Response** 26
Literature Model Allie's Basketball Dream
Student Model Story

Test Prep **LESSON 5 Writing Test Practice** 34

UNIT 2
WRITER'S CRAFT: ORGANIZATION

LESSON 1 Time-Order Words and Sequencing 38
Literature Model Turtle Bay
Student Model Directions

LESSON 2 Topic Sentence and Details 44
Literature Model Balto, The Dog Who Saved Nome
Student Model Paragraph of Information

LESSON 3 More About Topic Sentence and Details 50
Literature Model Wild Shots, They're My Life
Student Model Summary

Test Prep **LESSON 4 Review/Extended Written Response** 56
Literature Model Sue, the Tyrannosaurus Rex
Student Model How-to Essay

Test Prep **LESSON 5 Writing Test Practice** 64

UNIT 3
WRITER'S CRAFT: IDEAS

LESSON 1 Supporting an Opinion 68
Literature Model The Stories Julian Tells
Student Model Persuasive Paragraph

LESSON 2 Staying on Topic 74
Literature Model The Talent Show
Student Model Speech

LESSON 3 Reasons and Examples 80
Literature Model Centerfield Ballhawk
Student Model Persuasive Letter

Test Prep **LESSON 4 Review/Extended Written Response** 86
Literature Model Ramona Forever
Student Model Review

Test Prep **LESSON 5 Writing Test Practice** 94

UNIT 4
WRITER'S CRAFT:
SENTENCE FLUENCY

LESSON 1 Combining Sentences **98**
Literature Model Papa Tells Chita a Story
Student Model Paragraph That Compares

LESSON 2 Sentence Variety **104**
Literature Model Coyote Places the Stars
Student Model Paragraph That Contrasts

LESSON 3 More About Sentence Variety **110**
Literature Model Why Mosquitos Buzz in People's Ears
Student Model Paragraph that Explains

Test Prep **LESSON 4 Review/Extended Written Response** **116**
Literature Model Lon Po Po
Student Model Compare and Contrast Essay

Test Prep **LESSON 5 Writing Test Practice** **124**

UNIT 5
WRITER'S CRAFT:
ORGANIZATION

LESSON 1 Topic and Notes **128**
Literature Model Leah's Pony
Student Model Notes

LESSON 2 Organizing Information **134**
Literature Model Yippee-Yay!
Student Model Outline

LESSON 3 Writing a Research Draft **140**
Literature Model Boom Town
Student Model Draft

Test Prep **LESSON 4 Review/Extended Written Response** **146**
Literature Model Cocoa Ice
Student Model Edited Research Report

Test Prep **LESSON 5 Writing Test Practice** **154**

UNIT 6
WRITER'S CRAFT:
WORD CHOICE

LESSON 1 Imagery and Figurative Language **158**
Literature Model I'm in Charge of Celebrations
Student Model Poem

LESSON 2 Vivid Verbs **164**
Literature Model Alejandro's Gift
Student Model Thank-You Letter

LESSON 3 Using Vivid Verbs and Specific Nouns **170**
Literature Model Rocking and Rolling
Student Model Play

Test Prep **LESSON 4 Review/Extended Written Response** **176**
Literature Model The Armadillo from Amarillo
Student Model Invitation

Test Prep **LESSON 5 Writing Test Practice** **184**

CONVENTIONS

Writer's Grammar Guide **188**
Proofreader's Checklist **200**
Proofreader's Marks **201**

WRITER'S RESOURCES

Writing Across the Curriculum/Presentation **202**
Writer's Glossary of Terms **206**
Rubrics **207**

Introduction

When you first learn a new game, such as tennis or baseball, you usually are not very good at it. The more you play, the better you can become.

You can also get better at writing by doing it. This book will give you the skills, strategies, tips, and models you need to become the best writer you can be.

The Writing Process

Writing is a process in which you try different things and go through different steps. The writing process is often divided into five stages. Most writers go back and forth through the stages.

Prewriting

In this stage, you plan what you're going to write. You choose a topic and brainstorm ideas about it. You think of a good order for the ideas.

Drafting

In this stage, you put your ideas in writing as sentences and paragraphs. Follow your Prewriting plan to write a first draft.

Revising

In this stage, you may work by yourself or with a partner or group. Look over your writing, and see how you can make it clearer and stronger.

Proofreading

In this stage, you polish your work. Check for mistakes in grammar, spelling, capitalization, and punctuation. Make a final copy of your composition.

Publishing

Finally, you choose a way to present your work to others. You may want to add pictures, make a class book, or read your work aloud.

Writer's Craft and Writing Traits

You know that to play a game well, you need to use special skills and strategies. In baseball, for example, a player needs to hit well, catch well, and run quickly.

Good writing takes special skills and strategies, too. This web shows the traits, or characteristics, of good writing. You'll learn much more about these traits in this book.

The Traits of Good Writing

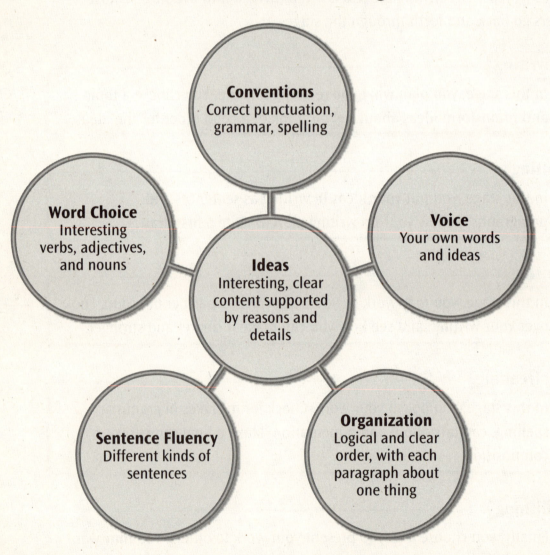

Traits Checklist

As you practice writing, ask yourself these questions.

☑ **FOCUS/IDEAS**	Is my purpose clear? Do I stay on the topic? Do I use details to support my ideas?
☑ **ORGANIZATION**	Are my ideas in a clear order? Do I have a beginning, a middle, and an ending? Are my ideas grouped in paragraphs? Do I use transitions, such as time-order words?
☑ **VOICE**	Do I use my own words and ideas? Do I seem to care about my topic and my audience?
☑ **WORD CHOICE**	Do I use specific nouns, strong verbs, and colorful adjectives?
☑ **SENTENCE FLUENCY**	Do I use different kinds of sentences?
☑ **CONVENTIONS**	Are my spelling, grammar, and punctuation correct?

© Harcourt

Writer's Companion
Introduction

LESSON 1: SENSORY DETAILS

Name _____

Writer's Craft in Literature

Look at Sensory Details

Sensory details help the reader hear, see, smell, taste, or feel what a writer is describing. Writers also use sensory details to show their feelings or **viewpoint**.

A. Read this passage. Notice how the writer uses sensory details to describe a big crowd.

Literature Model

Officer Buckle thought of a safety tip he had discovered that morning.

"NEVER leave a THUMBTACK where you might SIT on it!"

The audience roared. Officer Buckle grinned. He said the rest of the tips with *plenty* of expression.

The children clapped their hands and cheered. Some of them laughed until they cried."

—from *Officer Buckle and Gloria* by Peggy Rathman

B. Find the sensory details that make the story come alive. Some words will appeal to more than one sense.
1. Circle the words that describe what you can hear.
2. Put a box around words that describe what you can see.
3. Underline words that describe what you can feel or touch.

C. What words in the passage tell you that the audience enjoyed watching Officer Buckle and Gloria? Write them below.

_____

_____

_____

Writer's Companion • UNIT 1
Lesson 1 *Sensory Details*

8

LESSON 1: SENSORY DETAILS

Name _____

A Closer Look at Writer's Craft

Explore Sensory Details

Use **sensory details** to paint a clear picture when you write. Sensory details also help the reader know how you feel about your topic.

Sensory details help the reader see, hear, taste, smell, and feel what you are describing.	→ **Sensory details** can help you develop a strong personal voice in your writing. ←	**Sensory details** help the reader know how you feel about your topic.

A. Read each sentence. Then circle the senses that the details appeal to.

Example I gobbled up the sweet, juicy cherries.

        sound   (taste)   sight

1. I frowned at the gray, rainy sky.

        sight   touch   smell

2. The sweet scent of apple pie filled the house.

        smell   sight   touch

3. My head sunk into the soft pillow, and I fell fast asleep.

        touch   smell   sight

B. Read this sentence and underline the sensory details. Then answer the question.

    The slow rocking of the boat made Shawna sit back and relax.

How does Shawna feel? _____

C. Now imagine that Shawna gets sick on boats. Rewrite the sentence to show that she does not like being on the boat.

_____

_____

_____

© Harcourt

Writer's Companion • UNIT 1
Lesson 1 *Sensory Details*

LESSON 1: SENSORY DETAILS

Name _____

Practice with Writer's Craft

Use Sensory Details

Before you write about a sport, list some details that tell what you can see, taste, hear, smell, and feel at the game. Here is how one student started to think about her soccer game.

Example

See	Taste	Hear	Smell	Touch
• many people in the stands	• buttery	• loud cheering • whistle from referee	• popcorn	• clapped • retied

A. Think about a sport you have watched or played. Write its name on the line. Then fill out the chart.

Name of Sport: _____

See	Taste	Hear	Smell	Touch

B. Use information from your chart to write three sentences about a sport you have watched. Do your writing on another sheet of paper.

Writer's Companion • UNIT 1
Lesson 1 *Sensory Details*

10

© Harcourt

LESSON 1: SENSORY DETAILS

Name _____

Focus on the Writing Form

The Parts of a Descriptive Paragraph

A good **description** contains details that appeal to the senses. Here is a draft of a descriptive paragraph written by a third grader. As you read, think about how the student organized it. Then answer the questions.

Student Model

DRAFT

Goal!
by Ruby

This was the final game of the year. The stands were filled with people. Excited buyers surrounded the popcorn cart. My teammates nervously retied the laces of their cleats and checked their shin guards. They wanted the game to start. The referee threw the ball, and the game began. The crowd cheered loudly and clapped their hands. My friends waved bright, red banners with my jersey number on them. I took a deep breath and crouched down low in front of the goal. I was ready to play my best. I could almost taste the buttery popcorn.

> **Introduce** the topic in the first sentence.

> **Organize** your ideas in an order that makes sense.

> **Develop** your ideas by using sensory details that paint a picture of the scene.

1. Which sentence introduces the topic? Underline it.
2. Which sentence seems to be out of order? Circle it. Then draw an arrow to the place where you think this sentence belongs.
3. Find details that appeal to the senses. Write an example of each detail.

   see: _____   taste: _____

   hear: _____   touch: _____

4. What do the sensory details tell you about the game?

   _____

Writer's Grammar
Every sentence should begin with a capital letter and have an end mark. Check to be sure that all sentences in the model are written correctly.

Writer's Companion • UNIT 1
Lesson 1 *Sensory Details*

LESSON 1: SENSORY DETAILS

Name _____

Evaluating the Student Model

Evaluate a Descriptive Paragraph

When you evaluate a descriptive paragraph, ask yourself these questions:

- Does the writer use words that help you picture the scene?
  (Look for words that appeal to the five senses.)

- Does the writer organize details in a clear way?
  (Look for an order that makes sense.)

A. Reread the Student Model on page 11. Then follow the directions below.

  1. Name two sensory details that help you picture Ruby at the game.

  _____

  _____

  2. Give an example of a sensory detail that helps you picture the people in the stands.

  _____

B. Now evaluate the Student Model. Put a check in the box next to each thing the writer did well. If you do not think the writer did a good job, do not check the box.

☐ The writer introduced the topic at the beginning of the paragraph.
☐ All the sentences flow in a logical order.
☐ The writer included details that appeal to the senses.

C. How could the writer make the description better? Write your ideas below.

  _____

  _____

  _____

  _____

© Harcourt

Writer's Companion • UNIT 1
Lesson 1 *Sensory Details*

12

See the rubric on page 207 for another way to evaluate the Student Model.

LESSON 1: SENSORY DETAILS

Name _____

Revising the Student Model

Revise by Adding Details, Examples, and Transition Words

One thing the writer could have done better is to add details, examples, and transition words. Transition words such as *soon* or *first* help the reader keep track of ideas. Here is how a sentence from the Student Model can be improved.

Example   They wanted the game to start.

One member pulled on her shirt, another fidgeted with her

socks while waiting for the game to start.

A. Revise these sentences from the Student Model. Add details, examples, and transition words. Use the Word Bank to help you.

1. This was the final game of the year.

   _____

   _____

2. Excited buyers surrounded the popcorn cart.

   _____

   _____

3. The referee threw the ball, and the game began.

   _____

   _____

> **Word Bank**
>
> **sight**
> enormous
> trophy
> shiny
> brand-new
> **touch**
> reached
> carry
> bunted
> **transition words**
> finally
> near

B. Revise two of the sentences you wrote on page 10. Add details and use interesting, sensory words. If you need more space, use another sheet of paper.

_____

_____

© Harcourt

Writer's Companion • UNIT 1
Lesson 1 *Sensory Details*

13

LESSON 2: EXPRESSING YOUR VIEWPOINT

Name _____

**Writer's Craft
in Literature**

Look at Expressing Your Viewpoint

A **viewpoint** is a writer's thoughts and feelings about a subject. One way a
writer expresses his or her viewpoint is with colorful words that help the
reader know how the writer feels.

A. Read the passage. Notice how Pepita shows her feelings about her decision not to
speak Spanish anymore.

Literature Model

That night when she went to bed, Pepita pulled the blankets up to her
chin and made a stubborn face. "I'll find a way," she thought. "If I have to
I can call myself Pete. I can listen in Spanish. I can hum with the singing.
I can call a taco a crispy, crunchy, folded-over, round corn sandwich!
And Wolf will have to learn his name!" With that she turned over and
went to sleep.

—from *Pepita Talks Twice*
by Ofelia Dumas Lachtman

B. Find the words that the writer uses to show Pepita's viewpoint.
   1. Circle the actions showing that Pepita has made up her mind.
   2. Underline the colorful words that Pepita uses to describe a taco.

C. How did Pepita feel when she "went to sleep"?

_____

_____

Writer's Companion ▪ UNIT 1
Lesson 2 *Expressing Your Viewpoint*

14

© Harcourt

LESSON 2: EXPRESSING YOUR VIEWPOINT

Name _____

A Closer Look at Writer's Craft

Explore Expressing Your Viewpoint

Writers express their **viewpoint** through the words they choose. Colorful words help writers express viewpoints by painting pictures in the reader's mind.

| **Viewpoint** is how a writer feels about his or her subject. | → | **Express** thoughts, feelings, opinions, and experiences. | → | Paint pictures in the reader's mind with **colorful words.** |

A. Draw a box around colorful words that "paint a picture" or express a feeling.

Example I brushed the soft, feathery snow off my coat.

1. The rollercoaster ride made my stomach turn over.

2. I grew an oozing, green mold in science class.

3. I was safe and warm under the blanket.

B. Read this sentence. Then answer the question.

The beat of the music made the children spring to their feet.

How did the music make everyone feel? _____

_____

C. Use colorful words to describe how music makes you feel. You may need to use another sheet of paper.

_____

_____

_____

© Harcourt

Writer's Companion • UNIT 1
Lesson 2 *Expressing Your Viewpoint*

LESSON 2: EXPRESSING YOUR VIEWPOINT

Name _____

Practice with Writer's Craft

Use Expressing Your Viewpoint

In their journals and diaries, writers often express thoughts and feelings about events. They use colorful words. Here is how one student planned his writing about an unusual school day.

Example Event: <u>Show and Tell</u>

Colorful Words	Thoughts or Feelings
black and white pig red leather leash scrambled	scared excited

A. Think about something that happened one day during the past week. Write the topic of the event on the line. Then fill out the chart.

Event: _____

Colorful Words	Thoughts or Feelings

B. Use information from your chart to write a journal entry about the event that happened to you. Include colorful words to express your thoughts and feelings. Use another sheet of paper for your writing.

Writer's Companion • UNIT 1
Lesson 2 *Expressing Your Viewpoint*

16

© Harcourt

LESSON 2: EXPRESSING YOUR VIEWPOINT

Name _____

Focus on the Writing Form

The Parts of a Journal/Diary Entry

A **journal** or **diary entry** tells about events that happened. It should use colorful words to help express the writer's viewpoint. Here is a draft of a journal entry written by a third grader. As you read, think about how the student organized the entry. Then answer the questions.

DRAFT

**Journal Entry
by Darryl**

Friday, October 14

An unusual thing happened at school today. As I was finishing my math test, I saw Hans's mother at the door. She held a small black-and-white pig at the end of a red leather leash. I guess she was picking up Hans early. When Hans went to take the leash, he dropped it. The pig ran out of the classroom. The animal must have been scared. We all scrambled to the door to watch. Hans ran after the pig. "Daisy, come back!" he called. It sure would be fun to have a pig come to class more often.

Write the day and date of the entry.

Begin describing the event.

Use colorful words to explain what happened.

Make your viewpoint clear by including your thoughts and feelings about what happened.

1. Which sentence introduces the topic? Underline it.
2. Which sentence sums up Darryl's feelings? Put a box around it.
3. Find colorful words. Write them on the lines below.

_____

_____

Writer's Grammar
When telling about an event in the past, make sure that all the action words are in the past tense (*was, had*). Look for the action words in the Student Model that show what happened in the past.

17

Writer's Companion • UNIT 1
Lesson 2 *Expressing Your Viewpoint*

LESSON 2: EXPRESSING YOUR VIEWPOINT

Name _____

Evaluating the Student Model

Evaluate a Journal/Diary Entry

When you evaluate a journal entry, ask yourself these questions:

- Does the writer use colorful words to tell about events, thoughts, and feelings?
  (Look for the writer's viewpoint.)

- Does the writer organize details in a clear way?
  (Look for an order that makes sense.)

A. Reread the Student Model on page 17. Then follow the directions below.

1. List examples of colorful words that describe the pig.

_____

_____

2. Give an example of the writer's thoughts or feelings.

_____

_____

B. Now evaluate the Student Model. Put a check in the box next to each thing the writer has done well. If you do not think the writer did a good job, do not check the box.

☐ The day and date appear in the entry.
☐ All the sentences flow in a clear order.
☐ The writer included colorful words.
☐ The writer made his viewpoint clear by expressing thoughts and feelings.

C. How do you think the writer could make the journal entry better? Write your ideas below.

_____

_____

_____

Writer's Companion • UNIT 1
Lesson 2 *Expressing Your Viewpoint*

18

See the rubric on page 207 for another way to evaluate the Student Model.

© Harcourt

LESSON 2: EXPRESSING YOUR VIEWPOINT

Name _____

Revising the Student Model

Revise by Adding Important Details

One thing the writer could have done better is to add details to make the events clearer and more interesting. Here is one way the first sentence from the Student Model can be improved.

Example An unusual thing happened at school today.

I am usually very eager for Friday afternoon to come, but when the bell rang I didn't even want to move.

A. Revise these sentences from the Student Model by adding important or interesting details. Use the Word Bank to help you.

1. I saw Hans's mother at the door.

_____

_____

2. When Hans went to take the leash, he dropped it.

_____

_____

3. The animal must have been scared.

_____

_____

Word Bank

grab
leaped
little
looming
suddenly
suppose
terrified

_____
_____
_____
_____

B. Go ahead and revise the journal entry you wrote on page 16. Add details with colorful words. Do your writing on another sheet of paper.

© Harcourt

Writer's Companion • UNIT 1
Lesson 2 *Expressing Your Viewpoint*

LESSON 3: EXPRESSING FEELINGS

Name _____

Writer's Craft in Literature

Look at Expressing Feelings

Expressing feelings means telling how you feel about something or someone.

A. Read the model. Notice how Annie and Nate express their feelings during their phone call.

Literature Model

"Hello, Nate." It was Annie, from back home.

"We all miss you," she said. "And Fang has something to tell you."

I heard heavy breathing. I knew that Annie's dog, Fang, was on the line. I was happy to be many miles away from his teeth. I waited. Fang had nothing else to say. Then I heard a strange voice. It belonged to Rosamond.

—from *Nate the Great: San Francisco Detective*
by Marjorie Weinman Sharmat & Mitchell Sharmat

B. Find the words that the writer uses to show how Annie and Nate feel.
  1. Circle the words that show how Annie feels.
  2. Underline the words that Nate uses to describe how he feels.

C. When Annie says, "We all miss you," how do you think she feels?

_____

_____

Writer's Companion • UNIT 1
Lesson 3 *Expressing Feelings*

LESSON 3: EXPRESSING FEELINGS

Name _____

A Closer Look at Writer's Craft

Explore Expressing Feelings

Writers often express their personal voice by using "feeling" words such as *sad* or *joyful*. Writers also express their personal voice by describing their feelings indirectly.

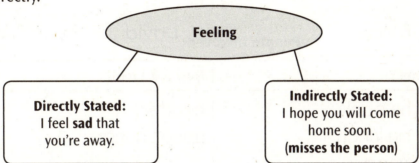

A. Read each sentence. Underline the "feeling" word or words.

   Example I was surprised to see so many people at the party.
   1. When the thunder woke me up last night, I was scared.
   2. I was annoyed because my little brother would just not stop yelling.
   3. He was upset since the school bus left without him.

B. Read these sentences. Then write a sentence to describe how the writer feels.

   It was the first day at my new school. I had butterflies in my stomach.

   _____
   _____

C. Think of a time you tried something new. Describe what you tried and how you felt about it. Use direct and indirect "feeling" words.

   _____
   _____
   _____

LESSON 3: EXPRESSING FEELINGS

Name _____

Practice with Writer's Craft

Use Expressing Feelings

Sometimes a writer tells about an event that really happened in his or her life. The writer also expresses feelings about the event. Here is how one third grader planned to write about a hike in the woods.

Example Event: _A Hike_   **People Involved:** _David, Justin, and Sam_

What happened?	How did I feel?
rode to the park	excited
dropped my lunch in the stream	upset, hungry
bug bites	itchy
wrong turn made the hike longer	tired

A. Think of a trip you have taken. Fill in the event and the people involved. Then complete the chart.

Event: _____ People Involved: _____

What happened?	How did I feel?

B. Use the information from your chart to write about your trip. Do your writing on another sheet of paper.

Writer's Companion • UNIT 1
Lesson 3 *Expressing Feelings*

22

© Harcourt

LESSON 3: EXPRESSING FEELINGS

Name _____

Focus on the Writing Form

The Parts of a Personal Narrative

A **personal narrative** tells about an event that happened to the writer. The narrative has a beginning, a middle, and an ending. Here is a draft of a personal narrative written by a third grader. As you read, think about how the student organized the draft. Then answer the questions.

Student Model

The Too-Long Hike
by David

Last Saturday, I went on a hike with Justin and his big brother, Sam. Sam drove us to Woodland Park. I was so excited about going!

On the trail, I tripped and dropped my lunch into the water. I was upset. I didn't have any lunch to eat.

Later, there was a place with lots of bugs. I got so many bug bites. Suddenly, I started itching badly.

We got to a fork in the trail, and Sam led us down the wrong path. It was an hour till we got back to the car. I was tired.

That was one hike I wasn't sorry to see end. It had been a too-long hike.

Introduce the topic. Write a topic sentence telling what your personal narrative is about.

Tell about the events. Tell only important events that happened on your trip. Write them down in order. Use time-order words to move the narrative along.

Express thoughts and feelings. Include interesting details, sensory descriptions, and words that show what the trip meant to you.

Have a strong ending. Summarize what made your trip special.

1. Which sentence introduces the topic? Underline it.
2. Which sentence tells how the writer felt before the hike? Draw a box around it.
3. Which sentences sum up the narrative? Circle them.

Writer's Grammar
A compound sentence is made up of two smaller sentences. It is joined by a word such as *and*, *but*, and *or*. Writers use a comma before the joining word. Look for a compound sentence in the Student Model.

Writer's Companion • UNIT 1
Lesson 3 *Expressing Feelings*

LESSON 3: EXPRESSING FEELINGS

Name _____

Evaluating the
Student
Model

Evaluate a Personal Narrative

When you evaluate a personal narrative, ask yourself these questions:

- Does the writer express his or her feelings?

- Does the narrative have a beginning, a middle, and an ending?

A. Reread the Student Model on page 23. Then answer these questions.

1. Give an example of feelings the writer expresses.

_____

_____

2. Why wasn't the writer sorry to see the hike end?

_____

_____

B. Now evaluate the Student Model. Put a check in the box next to each thing the writer has done well. If you do not think the writer did a good job, do not check the box.

☐ The writer introduced the topic in the first sentence.
☐ The writer told about the events in the order that they happened.
☐ The writer expressed his feelings clearly.
☐ The conclusion summarizes what made the trip special.

C. How do you think the writer could make the personal narrative better? Write your ideas below.

_____

_____

_____

_____

Writer's Companion • UNIT 1
Lesson 3 *Expressing Feelings*

24

See the rubric on page 207 for another way to evaluate the Student Model.

© Harcourt

LESSON 3: EXPRESSING FEELINGS

Name _____

Revising the Student Model

Revise by Expressing Feelings Clearly

One thing the writer could have done better is to add more words that show feelings. Here is an example of how a sentence from the Student Model can be improved.

Example   I was so excited about going!

I was so excited about going that I could hardly sit still.

A. Revise these sentences from the Student Model by adding "feeling" words. Use the Word Bank to help you.

1. I was upset.

_____

2. I didn't have any lunch to eat.

_____

3. Suddenly, I started itching badly.

_____

_____

4. It was an hour till we got back to the car.

_____

Word Bank

hungry
jump out of my skin
punched a tree
stomach growled
_____
_____
_____

B. Revise your writing on page 22. Add words that help you show your feelings clearly. If you need more space, use another sheet of paper.

_____

_____

_____

_____

© Harcourt

25

Writer's Companion • UNIT 1
Lesson 3 *Expressing Feelings*

LESSON 4: REVIEW VOICE

Name _____

**Writer's Craft
in Literature**

Review Voice

When writing, writers are careful to make their voices clear. They do
this by using **sensory details, colorful words,** and **words that express
feelings.**

A. Read the following passage. Notice how the writer expresses her voice.

Literature Model

Allie thought it over. She remembered the first time her father took her
to a basketball game at Madison Square Garden. She loved it all: The noise
of the crowd, the bright lights on the court, and especially the slam-dunks
the players made look so easy! She knew right then and there that one day,
she would be a professional basketball player too...

—from *Allie's Basketball Dream*
by Barbara E. Barber

B. Reread the passage. Look for sensory details that express the writer's voice clearly.
1. Underline a detail that tells about sight.
2. Circle a detail that tells about hearing.
3. Put a box around a detail that tells about touch.

C. How does the writer feel about basketball? Use details from the passage to help you
answer.

_____

_____

_____

Writer's Companion • UNIT 1
Lesson 4 *Review Voice*

26

© Harcourt

LESSON 4: REVIEW VOICE

Name _____

A Closer Look at Writer's Craft

Review Voice

Writers use **voice** to show what characters are like and how they feel.

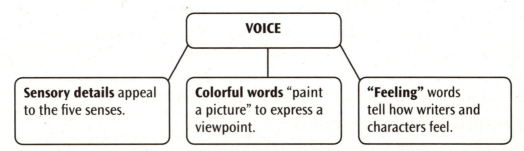

A. Read this beginning part of a story. Look for words and details that show what the characters are like and how they feel.

> Brianna sniffed the air as the muffins baked. They smelled so good her mouth watered. Only ten more minutes to wait. She could almost taste the sweet, tangy blueberries. She put on a CD to make the time go faster. The beat was loud and thumping. Brianna danced joyfully around the room. The music was so loud that she didn't hear the timer go off. She danced and danced, lost in the music. Suddenly, she stopped. A strong, smoky smell made her cough. Black smoke was coming from the kitchen. Something was on fire!

B. Write the details that appeal to each sense.

Example smell: They smelled so good her mouth watered.

1. hearing: _____
2. smell: _____
3. sight: _____

C. How does Brianna feel when she is dancing? Which colorful and "feeling" words tell you this?

_____

_____

LESSON 4: REVIEW VOICE

Name _____

Practice with Writer's Craft

Review Voice

When you write a story, you create characters. You can use voice to show what the characters are like and how they feel. Read the example in the box below. It shows how one third grader began to use voice to create a character.

> **Felix has forgotten to pick up his little brother after preschool.**
>
> **Sensory Details:** dark streets, cold rain
>
> **Colorful Words:** terrible sinking feeling, tearstained face
>
> **"Feeling" Words:** worried, scared, relieved

A. Read the sentence below. Then think of words and details to add that can show how the character feels. Write your sentences on the lines.

> Keisha climbed too far up in the tree.

1. Write a sensory detail to show how the tree bark might feel to Keisha.

_____

_____

2. Write a sentence with colorful words or "feeling" words to show that Keisha is afraid.

_____

_____

B. Write three or four sentences that describe how Keisha tries to get down from the tree. Include sensory details, colorful words, and "feeling" words. If you need more space, use another sheet of paper.

_____

_____

_____

_____

Writer's Companion • UNIT 1
Lesson 4 *Review Voice*

28

LESSON 4: REVIEW VOICE

Name _____

Focus on the Writing Form

The Parts of a Story

In this unit you have learned how writers use voice to show their own feelings and those of their characters. But a **story** has more than just a writer's voice. A story includes characters, a setting, and a plot. Below is a first draft of a story written by a third grader. As you read, think about how the student organized the story and also used voice to show how the characters feel. Then answer the questions.

Student Model

DRAFT

Felix Forgets
by Marcos

While waiting in the park, Felix fell asleep. Suddenly, he opened his eyes. He looked at his watch. It was five o'clock. He had a terrible sinking feeling. He had forgotten to pick up Ramon after preschool!

Felix sprang to his feet. He raced through the dark, wet streets. As he ran, he worried about his brother. Felix imagined his tear stained face. Ramon was only four. Ramon would never forgive him. Felix felt terribly guilty.

Felix burst through the door of the preschool. The teacher looked up from her desk and smiled. There was Ramon, happily playing with toy cars. He saw his brother and grinned. Felix melted at the sight. "Hey, Felix," Ramon shouted. "You are *late!*"

> **Introduce** the setting, characters, and problem.

> **Organize** events in the order they happened.

> **Provide** details. Give sensory details that create mental pictures.

> **Create** a strong ending. Explain how the main character solved the problem.

> **TIP:** Use a mix of different types of sentences in a story. Include statements, exclamations, questions, and commands.

1. Underline the sentence that introduces Felix.
2. Draw [ ] around the sentence that tells Felix's problem.
3. Circle the sentences that tell how Felix feels about his problem.
4. In your own words, tell how Felix feels at the end of the story.

© Harcourt

Writer's Companion • UNIT 1
Lesson 4 *Review Voice*

29

LESSON 4: REVIEW VOICE

Name _____

Evaluating the Student Model

Evaluate a Story

A. Two students were asked to write a story about a person who faces a problem. The story below got a score of 4. When using a 4-point rubric, a score of 4 means "excellent." Read the story and the teacher comments that go with it. Find out why this story is a success.

> ### Student Model
>
> DRAFT
>
> ### The Scary Dog
> ### by Diana
>
> Anna had always been afraid of dogs. It didn't matter if they were big or little. Even their wagging tails scared her. So when she saw the puppy on the sidewalk, she thought about crossing the street. Then she noticed it was shaking. Its head and tail were down. It was so thin that Anna could count its ribs.
>
> Anna stopped near the puppy. It had that "wet dog" smell. It wasn't too terrible, though. The puppy was the saddest-looking thing she had ever seen.
>
> "Hey, pup," she said softly. "Don't you have a home?"
>
> The puppy looked up and wagged, just a little. Carefully Anna reached down and held out her hand. Her heart beat very hard. The puppy came nearer. Nervously, it touched its nose to Anna's hand. Then it licked her. The rough feel of its tongue made Anna smile.
>
> "I guess you should come with me," she told the puppy. "How does a bath and dinner sound to you?"
>
> The puppy wagged so hard it nearly fell over. Anna laughed. She knew she would never be afraid of dogs again.

Nice beginning! You tell about the main character, the setting, and the problem here.

This detail appeals to the sense of smell.

These colorful and "feeling" words tell how Anna feels. Good!

This detail appeals to the sense of touch.

Your ending is strong. Anna's problem is solved!

© Harcourt

Writer's Companion • UNIT 1
Lesson 4 *Review Voice*

30

LESSON 4: REVIEW VOICE

Name _____

Evaluating the Student Model

B. This paragraph got a score of 2. Why did it get a low score?

Student Model

DRAFT

The Test
by Jennifer

Callie knew something was wrong. The classroom was quite. All the students were at their desks. Mr. Boland stood at the front of the room. He looked very serious. Callie sat down quickly. At her desk. It was the big test. Mr. Boland passed out booklets. She had forgotten. What could she do? "Mr. Boland, I forgot we were having the test today," Callie said to the teacher.

Mr. Boland smiled. "You also forgot what I said. It isn't the kind of test you can study for. Don't worry, Callie. Just do your best."

Callie looked at the booklet on her desk. She felt a little better.

> Your opening is interesting, but there are some spelling and sentence construction errors.

> You have not told how Callie feels about forgetting.

> Some details that appeal to the senses might be good here.

> Your ending does not tell what happened to Callie.

C. What score would you give the student's story? Put a number on each line.

	4	3	2	1
Voice _____	☐ The writer uses many colorful and feeling words.	☐ The writer uses some colorful and feeling words.	☐ The writer uses few or no colorful and feeling words.	☐ The writer does not show the characters' feelings.
Sensory Details _____	☐ The writer uses sensory details.	☐ The writer uses some sensory details.	☐ The writer uses few sensory details.	☐ The writer uses no sensory details.
Organization _____	☐ There is a beginning, middle, and ending. Events are in order.	☐ There are characters and a problem. Some events are in order.	☐ The problem is unclear. Events may be out of order.	☐ The writer has used no organizing structure.

© Harcourt

Writer's Companion ▪ UNIT 1
Lesson 4 *Review Voice*

LESSON 4: REVIEW VOICE

Name _____

Extended Writing/Test Prep

Extended Writing/Test Prep

On the last two pages of this lesson, you will use what you have learned to write a longer written work.

A. **Read the three choices below. Put a star by the writing activity you would like to do.**

1. Respond to a Writing Prompt

Writing Situation: Everyone has faced a problem in life.

Directions for Writing: Think about a problem facing someone.

Now write about someone who is facing a problem. Use sensory details, colorful words, and "feeling" words to show how characters feel.

2. Choose one of the pieces of writing you started in this unit:

- a descriptive paragraph (page 10)
- a journal/diary entry (page 16)
- a personal narrative (page 22)

Expand your draft into a complete piece of writing. Use what you have learned about voice.

3. Choose a topic you would like to write about. You may write a journal/diary entry, a personal narrative, or a story. Use voice to help your writing come alive.

B. **Use the space below and on the next page to plan your writing.**

TOPIC: _____

_____

WRITING FORM: _____

HOW WILL I ORGANIZE MY WRITING: _____

_____

Writer's Companion • UNIT 1
Lesson 4 *Review Voice*

© Harcourt

LESSON 4: REVIEW VOICE

Name _____

Extended Writing/Test Prep

C. In the space below, draw a graphic organizer that will help you plan your writing. Fill in the graphic organizer. Write more notes on the lines below.

Notes

_____

_____

_____

_____

_____

_____

_____

D. Do your writing on another sheet of paper.

33

Writer's Companion • UNIT 1
Lesson 4 *Review Voice*

LESSON 5: WRITING TEST PRACTICE

Name _____

Writing Test Practice

Answering Multiple-Choice Questions

A. For some multiple-choice questions, you will have to read a passage with numbered sentences. Read the test tip. Then practice this type of question.

Read the passage. Then read each question and fill in the correct answer on your Answer Sheet.

Who Is There?

(1) It had gotten dark fast. (2) Delia walked quickly. (3) Then she heard a voice next to her ask, "Who." (4) Delia screamed. (5) She cried, "Who is there (6) Come out right now" (7) Again the voice said, "Who?" (8) Then wings flapped. (9) Delia saw an owl fly off into the woods.

1. What change, if any, should be made in sentence 5?

   F   Add a question mark after *there*

   G   Add a period after *there*

   H   Add an exclamation point after *there*

   I   Make no change

2. What change, if any, should be made in sentence 6?

   A   Add a question mark after *now*

   B   Add a comma after *now*

   C   Add an exclamation point after *now*

   D   Make no change

3. What change, if any, should be made in sentence 9?

   F   Change *woods.* to **woods?**

   G   Change *woods.* to **woods!**

   H   Insert a period after *owl*

   I   Make no change

Test Tip:
Use this rhyme to help you use the correct punctuation:

Would you like to be my friend? A question mark is the way to end.

I'd like to be your friend indeed. A period is what I need.

Answer all test questions on this Answer Sheet.	
1. Ⓕ Ⓖ Ⓗ Ⓘ	3. Ⓕ Ⓖ Ⓗ Ⓘ
2. Ⓐ Ⓑ Ⓒ Ⓓ	

Writer's Companion • UNIT 1
Lesson 5 *Writing Test Practice*

© Harcourt

LESSON 5: WRITING TEST PRACTICE

Name _____

Writing Test Practice

B. For some multiple-choice questions, you will have to read a passage and then decide the best way to correct a sentence. Read the test tip. Then practice answering this kind of question on the Answer Sheet below.

The following is a rough draft of a student's personal narrative. It may contain errors. Look for errors as you read it.

In the Desert

(1) Every spring I visit my grandparents in San Diego. (2) we always go for a walk in the desert (3) This year all the flowers were in bloom. (4) It was very beautiful. (5) I saw something move as we walked? (6) It was a snake. (7) "Watch out!" my grandma cried. (8) "that's a rattlesnake" (9) We watched it slither away. (10) It was our best desert walk ever.

1. How should sentence 2 be correctly written?
   A we always go for a walk in the desert.
   B We always go for a walk in the desert
   C We always go for a walk in the desert.
   D we always go for a walk in the desert?

2. How should sentence 5 be correctly written?
   A I saw something move as we walked?
   B I saw something move as we walked.
   C i saw something move as we walked.
   D I saw something move as we walked,

3. How should sentence 8 be correctly written?
   A "That's a rattlesnake!"
   B "That's a rattlesnake?"
   C "that's a rattlesnake?"
   D "That's a rattlesnake"!

Test Tip:
A complete sentence must begin with a capital letter and end with an end mark.

Answer all test questions on this Answer Sheet.

1. Ⓐ Ⓑ Ⓒ Ⓓ   3. Ⓐ Ⓑ Ⓒ Ⓓ
2. Ⓐ Ⓑ Ⓒ Ⓓ

Writer's Companion • UNIT 1
Lesson 5 *Writing Test Practice*

LESSON 5: WRITING TEST PRACTICE

Name _____

Writing Test Practice

C. For some writing tests, you will have to answer questions based on a graphic organizer. Follow the directions to practice answering this kind of question. Use the test tip to help you.

Noah made the plan below to organize ideas for a paper. Read his plan to answer questions 1–3.

Topic: _My Entry into an Art Contest_

	Beginning	**Middle**	**End**
What happened?	I painted a picture. I like to draw, too.	I entered the picture in an art contest at school.	I won second place. I got a silver ribbon.
How did I feel?	excited	scared, nervous	disappointed proud

1. Based on the information in Noah's writing plan, what is Noah planning to write?
   - (A) a research report
   - (B) a news article
   - (C) a personal narrative
   - (D) a how-to paragraph

2. Which detail is off topic and should be taken out of Noah's writing plan?
   - (F) I entered the picture in an art contest.
   - (G) I won second place.
   - (H) I got a silver ribbon.
   - (I) I like to draw, too.

3. Which detail should be placed in the box labeled "End"?
   - (A) Alex Cody won first place.
   - (B) The picture was of a lake.
   - (C) The art contest was on Tuesday.
   - (D) My class liked my painting.

Test Tip: Events in a writing plan should be in time order.

© Harcourt

Writer's Companion • UNIT 1
Lesson 5 _Writing Test Practice_

36

LESSON 5: WRITING TEST PRACTICE

Name _____

Writing Test Practice

D. For some multiple-choice questions, you will have to read sentences and then decide the best way to combine and order them. Read the test tip and the questions. Then fill in the circle next to the correct answer.

1. Combine the sentences in the box to make one sentence.

> Mollie takes dance lessons.
> Avram takes dance lessons.

Which sentence correctly combines the sentences in the box?

Ⓐ Mollie takes and Avram takes dance lessons.

Ⓑ Mollie and Avram take dance lessons.

Ⓒ Mollie takes dance lessons and Avram takes dance lessons.

2. Combine the sentences in the box to make one sentence.

> The dog chased the ball.
> The dog caught the ball.

Which sentence correctly combines the sentences in the box?

Ⓕ The dog and the dog chased and caught the ball.

Ⓖ The dog chased the ball and the dog caught the ball.

Ⓗ The dog chased and caught the ball.

3. Combine the sentences in the box to make one sentence.

> Lexie went to the store.
> Lexie bought a notebook.

Which sentence correctly combines the sentences in the box?

Ⓐ Lexie went to the store and bought a notebook.

Ⓑ Lexie went and she bought a notebook to the store.

Ⓒ Lexie went to the store and Lexie bought a notebook.

Test Tip:

• You can combine sentences with the same subject by combining predicates.

• You can combine sentences with the same predicate by combining subjects.

© Harcourt

37

Writer's Companion • UNIT 1
Lesson 5 *Writing Test Practice*

LESSON 1: TIME-ORDER WORDS AND SEQUENCING

Name _____

Writer's Craft in Literature

Look at Time-Order Words and Sequencing

As you read, it is important to keep track of the order of the events. Writers use time-order words such as *now, first, next,* and *last* to tell us when things happen in a story.

A. Read the following Literature Model. Notice how the writer uses time-order words to tell you the order of events.

> The three friends swept up all the litter dropped by the beachgoers during the day. Then they sat on the rocks and watched more turtles coming ashore. There were lots of them—all huge and old and wise—just like Jiro-San.
>
> "Now," said Jiro-San, "you must be patient, and wait to hear from me again."
>
> Eight weeks later, Jiro-San told the children to meet him at dusk.
>
> —from *Turtle Bay* by Saviour Pirotta

B. Identify the words that tell you the order of events.
1. Underline the sentence that tells you what the friends did *after* they swept up the litter.
2. Circle the time-order word in the sentence you underlined.

C. Write the answers to the questions on the lines.
1. Which words in the passage tell you how long it took to hear from Jiro-San again?

   _____

2. At what time of day will Jiro-San meet the children?

   _____

Writer's Companion • UNIT 2
Lesson 1 *Time-Order Words and Sequencing*

LESSON 1: TIME-ORDER WORDS AND SEQUENCING

Name _____

A Closer Look at Writer's Craft

Explore Time-Order Words and Sequencing

Writers use words such as *before*, *next*, and *a day later* to show **time order** or **sequence**.

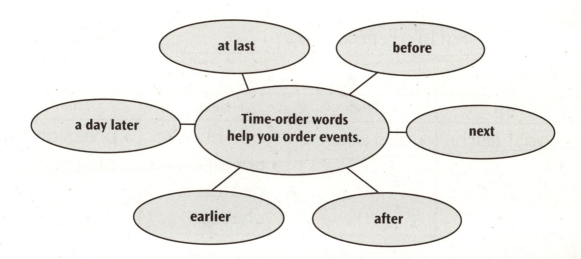

A. Underline the time-order word or words in each sentence. Then circle the event that happened first.

Example   I always eat my toast after I eat my eggs.

1. Make sure to prepare all the ingredients before you start to cook.

2. First I heard a crack of thunder, and later I saw lightning.

3. I did my homework and then watched some TV.

B. Read these sentences from *Turtle Bay*, and underline the time-order word.

> The boy and the old man swept the beach from one end to the other. They collected all the rubbish and put it in Jiro-San's cart. Soon the beach was cleaner than it had been all summer.

C. What was the second thing the boy and the old man did? Write your answer on the lines.

_____

_____

Writer's Companion • UNIT 2
Lesson 1 *Time-Order Words and Sequencing*

LESSON 1: TIME-ORDER WORDS AND SEQUENCING

Name _____

Practice with Writer's Craft

Use Time-Order Words and Sequencing

Before you write directions, make sure you know the order of the steps.
Here is how one student planned a recipe for her favorite snack.

Example

Name of Snack: Patty's Perfect Pizza

First	Then	Next	Finally
• toast muffin	• add sauce	• add cheese • sprinkle grated cheese	• press and pull apart

A. Think about a snack you like to make. Name the snack. Then fill out the chart.

Name of Snack: _____

First	Then	Next	Finally

B. Use information from your chart to write directions that explain how to make your snack. Use another sheet of paper, if you need to.

_____

_____

_____

Writer's Companion • UNIT 2
Lesson 1 *Time-Order Words and Sequencing*

LESSON 1: TIME-ORDER WORDS AND SEQUENCING

Name _____

Focus on the Writing Form

The Parts of Directions

Good **directions** give the steps of a task in time order. The paragraph below is a first draft of a recipe that was written by a third grader. As you read, think about how the student organized the steps. Then answer the questions.

Student Model

DRAFT

Patty's Perfect Pizza
by Patty

Here's a great way to make your own pizza. First, divide an English muffin in half and toast it. Put the two halves you just toasted on a plate. Spread a little tomato sauce on each half. Before you start, get together the ingredients. Next, unwrap a couple of pieces of sliced cheese, put the cheese slices on top of the sauce, and then sprinkle some grated cheese on top. Then, press the two halves together. You have to press for about five seconds. The cheese will have a chance to melt. At last, pull the halves apart carefully and put the halves back on the same plate you had at the beginning.

> **Introduce** the topic with a sentence that clearly states the task.

> **Organize** the steps in time order using sequence words.

> **Include details** readers need to know to complete the task.

1. Which sentence introduces the topic? Put a box around it.
2. Underline the sentence that tells what to do last.
3. Which sentence seems to be out of order? Circle it. Then draw an arrow to the place where you think this sentence belongs.
4. Find the time-order words. Write them below.

_____

5. How do time-order words help you with the recipe?

_____

Writer's Grammar

You can join two complete sentences to make a compound sentence. Join the sentences with a comma followed by *and* or *but*. "I ran home, and then I came back," is a compound sentence. Find a compound sentence in the Student Model.

Writer's Companion • UNIT 2
Lesson 1 *Time-Order Words and Sequencing*

LESSON 1: TIME-ORDER WORDS AND SEQUENCING

Name _____

Evaluating the Student Model

Evaluate Directions

When you evaluate directions, ask yourself these questions:

- Does the writer put the steps in the correct sequence?
  (Look for time-order words such as *before, first, next,* and *finally*.)

- Does the writer include clear, easy to follow directions?
  (Look for details that give important information, such as how long
  the halves should be pressed together.)

A. Reread the Student Model on page 41. Then answer these questions.

1. Write two sentences from the model that contain time-order words. Circle the
   time-order words.

   _____

   _____

2. What happens after the grated cheese is added?

   _____

**B. Now evaluate the Student Model. Put a check in the box next to each thing the writer
has done well. If you do not think the writer did a good job with something, do not
check the box.**

- ☐ The first sentence clearly states the task.
- ☐ The materials are listed in order near the beginning.
- ☐ The writer used a straightforward tone.
- ☐ The writer used details that give important information.
- ☐ The writer put sentences in sequence order.
- ☐ The writer used time-order words to help sequence the steps.

C. How do you think the writer could make the directions better?

_____

_____

Writer's Companion • UNIT 2
Lesson 1 *Time-Order Words and Sequencing*

42

See the rubric on page 207 for another
way to evaluate the Student Model.

© Harcourt

LESSON 1: TIME-ORDER WORDS AND SEQUENCING

Name _____

Revising the Student Model

Revise by Deleting

One thing the student writer could have done better is to delete unnecessary words and details. Here is an example of how a sentence from the Student Model can be improved.

Example   **Original:** At last, pull the halves apart carefully and put the halves back on the same plate you had at the beginning.

Revision: At last, pull the halves apart carefully and put them back on the plate.

A. Revise these sentences from the Student Model. Delete unimportant details.

1. Put the two halves you just toasted on a plate.

_____

_____

2. Next, unwrap a couple of pieces of sliced cheese, put the cheese slices on top of the sauce, and then sprinkle some grated cheese on top.

_____

_____

3. Then, press the two halves together. You have to press for about five seconds.

_____

_____

B. Revise two of the sentences you wrote on page 40. Delete unnecessary words and details. Use more paper if necessary.

_____

_____

_____

© Harcourt

Writer's Companion • UNIT 2
Lesson 1 *Time-Order Words and Sequencing*

LESSON 2: TOPIC SENTENCE AND DETAILS

Name _____

Writer's Craft in Literature

Look at Topic Sentence and Details

The **topic sentence** of a paragraph tells you the main idea. The sentences that follow give examples with **details** that support the main idea.

A. Read the following passage. Notice how the writer uses a topic sentence and supporting details to give you information about a subject.

Literature Model

The first part of the trail to Nome led across sea ice. The ice wasn't anything like ice on a small pond or lake. It seemed much more *alive*. And no wonder. The water *under* the ice was moving up and down because of the storm. So the ice was moving up and down too. Up and down, up and down it went, like a roller coaster.

—from "Balto, the Dog Who Saved Nome," *Seven True Dog Stories* by Margaret Davidson

B. Identify the words that tell you the topic sentence and details.
   1. Underline the topic sentence.
   2. Circle one sentence that gives information about the main idea.

C. Which words in the topic sentence tell you what the rest of the passage is about? Write them below.

_____

Writer's Companion • UNIT 2
Lesson 2 *Topic Sentence and Details*

LESSON 2: TOPIC SENTENCE AND DETAILS

Name _____

A Closer Look at Writer's Craft

Explore Topic Sentence and Details

Writers use a **topic sentence** to present the main idea. They use **details** to give examples and information about the main idea.

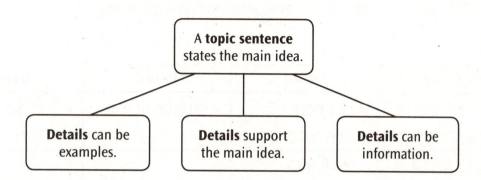

A. Underline the topic sentence, or main idea. Circle the sentence that does not support the topic.

Example Dogs help people in many ways. Some work as seeing-eye dogs. Some, like sled dogs, pull heavy loads. Other dogs help people in wheel chairs. I love my dog Charlie very much.

1. Fall is my favorite season. The leaves turn colors. The air turns brisk. Summer is my next-favorite season. Fall air smells like winter is on the way.

2. The storm was very scary. First, lightning lit up the sky. Then, after about five seconds of silence, I heard a low rumbling. Heavy rain continued as more lightning struck. The red truck slowed down on the highway.

B. Read these sentences from "Balto, the Dog Who Saved Nome." Underline the topic sentence. Circle three details that support the topic.

The teams were ready. The first team pushed north through the storm to a little town. There a second team was waiting. It went on to another small town where a third team was ready to take the medicine farther.

C. Suppose you are writing "Balto, the Dog Who Saved Nome." Add another detail to the paragraph above. Make sure it supports the topic sentence.

_____

_____

LESSON 2: TOPIC SENTENCE AND DETAILS

Name _____

Practice with Writer's Craft

Use Topic Sentence and Details

Before you write a paragraph of information, make sure you have a topic sentence and enough details to support it. Here is how one student planned a paragraph of information about what makes a good pet.

Example My Pet _Cat_____

Topic Sentence	Detail	Detail	Detail
• I think cats are the best pets to have.	• do not have to be walked	• mysterious	• fun to watch

A. Think about a pet you would like to have. Write what animal it is on the line. Then fill out the chart.

My Pet: _____

Topic Sentence	Detail	Detail	Detail

B. Use information from your chart. Write a paragraph to explain why the animal you chose would make a good pet. Use more paper if you need it.

_____

_____

_____

Writer's Companion • UNIT 2
Lesson 2 *Topic Sentence and Details*

© Harcourt

LESSON 2: TOPIC SENTENCE AND DETAILS

Name _____

Focus on the Writing Form

The Parts of a Paragraph of Information

A **paragraph of information** gives a topic sentence followed by details or examples to support it. Below is a draft of a paragraph written by a third grader. As you read, think about how the student organized her paragraph. Then answer the questions.

Student Model

DRAFT

Cats Are Cool
by Jessie

I think cats are the best pets to have. They are quiet and cute. They sleep on your bed. Also, they are fun to watch, and I love to watch them. Buster is two years old, and I got him at a shelter. Cats are very mysterious, but some people say dogs are too. They will do crazy things for no reason at all. They don't need to be walked, but they do have to have food and water. For instance, they will suddenly leap up and twirl around. They will stare for hours out the kitchen window or the bedroom window. You never know what cats are thinking. I love my cat Buster very much. If you get a cat you will not be sorry.

Introduce the topic by writing a sentence that clearly states the main idea of the pararagraph.

Organize the supporting details by deciding on an order that makes sense.

Develop your idea by writing sentences that present the details in the order you chose.

Conclude by writing a last sentence that restates the main idea.

1. What is the topic sentence of the paragraph? Underline it.
2. Which sentence repeats the main idea of the paragraph? Put a box around it.
3. Which sentence seems unnecessary? Circle it.

Writer's Grammar

A **common noun** names a person, place, or thing. A **proper noun** names a particular person, place, or thing. Make sure you begin each proper noun with a capital letter. Find a common noun and a proper noun in the model.

LESSON 2: TOPIC SENTENCE AND DETAILS

Name _____

Evaluating the Student Model

Evaluate a Paragraph of Information

When you evaluate a paragraph of information, ask yourself these questions:

- Does the paragraph have a clear topic sentence?
  (Look for a topic sentence that clearly states the main idea.)

- Does the writer include examples supporting the main idea?
  (Look for details that give information about the topic.)

A. Reread the Student Model on page 47. Then follow the directions below.

   1. Name two details that tell why cats make the best pets.

    _____

    _____

   2. Give an example of a detail that supports the idea that cats are mysterious.

    _____

    _____

B. Now evaluate the Student Model. Put a check in the box next to each thing the writer has done well. If you do not think the writer did a good job with something, do not check the box.

- ☐ The writer included a topic sentence that clearly states the main idea.
- ☐ The detail sentences give examples that support the main idea.
- ☐ The writer put sentences in an order that makes sense.
- ☐ The conclusion restates the main idea of the paragraph.

C. How do you think the writer could make the paragraph better?

_____

_____

_____

Writer's Companion • UNIT 2
Lesson 2 *Topic Sentence and Details*

See the rubric on page 207 for another way to evaluate the Student Model.

© Harcourt

LESSON 2: TOPIC SENTENCE AND DETAILS

Name _____

Revising the Student Model

Revise by Deleting

One thing the student writer could have done better is to delete details that do not fit or are not important. Here is an example of how a sentence from the Student Model can be improved by deleting unnecessary details.

Example   **Original:** Cats are very mysterious, but some people say dogs are too.

Revision: _Cats are very mysterious._

A. Revise these sentences from the Student Model. Delete unimportant details and combine sentences when necessary.

1. Also, they are fun to watch, and I love to watch them.

   _____

   _____

2. They will stare for hours out the kitchen window or the bedroom window.

   _____

   _____

3. They are quiet and cute. They sleep on your bed.

   _____

   _____

B. Revise the paragraph you wrote on page 46. Delete any words that are unimportant or do not support the topic. Continue on another sheet of paper.

   _____

   _____

   _____

   _____

© Harcourt

49

Writer's Companion ▪ UNIT 2
Lesson 2 *Topic Sentence and Details*

LESSON 3: MORE ABOUT TOPIC SENTENCE AND DETAILS

Name _____

Writer's Craft in Literature

Look at More About Topic Sentence and Details

The topic sentence of a paragraph tells you the main idea. Other sentences in a paragraph usually give details that support the main idea.

A. Read the following paragraph. As you read, look for the main idea and the details.

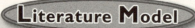

> The Galapagos Islands are famous for their huge tortoises. In fact, *galapagos* means "tortoises" in Spanish. When early Spanish-speaking explorers came to the islands, they saw *tons* of these big fellas.
>
> —from "Wild Shots, They're My Life" *Ranger Rick* Magazine by Tui De Roy

B. Identify the topic sentence and details.
  1. Underline the topic sentence.
  2. Circle the main idea in the topic sentence.
  3. Put a box around a detail that tells about the main idea.

C. Write another detail.

_____

_____

_____

LESSON 3: MORE ABOUT TOPIC SENTENCE AND DETAILS

Name _____

A Closer Look at Writer's Craft

Explore More About Topic Sentence and Details

A **topic sentence** tells the main idea of a paragraph. **Detail** sentences use key words to give information about the main idea.

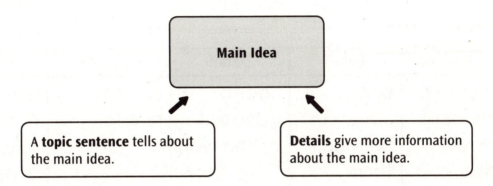

A. Read each pair of sentences. Underline the topic sentence that tells the main idea. Circle one or more key words that support the main idea.

Example Here's a great snack. Spread (peanut butter) on a (banana!)

1. The school picnic was fun. We played games and ate lunch.

2. A new zoo is planned for the city. There will be a farm and a petting zoo.

B. Read this sentence from "Wild Shots, They're My Life." Circle the details that tell about "my best friends."

When I was a little girl, all my best friends were furry, feathered, or scaly!

C. Write two details about your best friend.

_____

_____

Writer's Companion • UNIT 2
Lesson 3 *More About Topic Sentence and Details*

LESSON 3: MORE ABOUT TOPIC SENTENCE AND DETAILS

Name _____

Practice with Writer's Craft

Use More About Topic Sentence and Details

A summary is a short form of a longer piece of writing. A summary includes a main idea and the most important details. When you write a summary, use your own words. Here is how one third grader planned her summary.

Example Name of Animal: _Tortoise_

Topic Sentence	Detail	Detail	Detail	Detail
The writer was nose to nose with a tortoise.	only a camera between them	had to move out of the way	eating plants	bent down to take the picture

A. Think about an animal you have observed. Name the animal and fill out the chart.

Name of Animal: _____

Topic Sentence	Detail	Detail	Detail	Detail

B. Write a summary of the most important information from your chart. Include a topic sentence and details. Use another sheet of paper for your writing.

Writer's Companion • UNIT 2
Lesson 3 *More About Topic Sentence and Details*

52

© Harcourt

LESSON 3: MORE ABOUT TOPIC SENTENCE AND DETAILS

Name _____

Focus on the Writing Form

The Parts of a Summary

When you write a **summary** from a longer piece of writing, always begin with a topic sentence. Then include only the most important ideas. Below is the first draft of a summary written by a third grader. As you read, think about how the student organized the summary. Then answer the questions.

Student Model

DRAFT

Summary
by Rachel

The writer was nose to nose with a big tortoise. There was just a camera between them. The tortoise didn't notice her there. She had to move out of the animal's way before it bumped right into her! It must have been so scary. The tortoise was busy eating tasty plants. Tortoises don't mind the spines of a cactus. Then the writer bent down and snapped the picture. The picture was great. The writer said getting close is the best way to get great action shots. CHOMP!

> **Write** a topic sentence that tells the main idea.

> **Choose the most important ideas or details** from the longer selection. Restate them in your own words.

> **Leave out** less important opinions and details.

> Put your **ideas in an order** that makes sense. Follow the order of the ideas in the selection you are summarizing.

1. What sentence tells the main idea of the summary? Underline it.
2. Which sentence gives an important idea? Put a box around it.
3. Circle a detail.
4. Put [ ] around an opinion.

© Harcourt

Writer's Grammar
Most of the time you add *–ed* to a verb (action word) to change the action to the past: *jump–jumped*. Other times, the past form of a verb changes in a different, or irregular, way: *send–sent*. Find past forms of verbs in the Student Model.

Writer's Companion • UNIT 2
Lesson 3 *More About Topic Sentence and Details*

53

LESSON 3: MORE ABOUT TOPIC SENTENCE AND DETAILS

Name _____

Evaluating the Student Model

Evaluate a Summary

When you evaluate a summary, ask yourself these questions:

- Does the summary begin with a sentence that tells the main idea?
  (Look for a sentence that clearly states the main idea.)

- Does the summary include only the most important ideas?
  (Make sure there are no opinions or details.)

A. **Reread the Student Model on page 53. Then follow the directions below.**

    1. Name two important ideas from the summary.

    _____

    _____

    2. Give two unimportant details from the summary.

    _____

    _____

B. **Now evaluate the Student Model. Put a check in the box next to each thing the writer has done well. If you do not think the writer did a good job with something, do not check the box.**

    ☐ The writer began with a sentence that clearly states the main idea of the summary.

    ☐ The sentences that follow give only the most important ideas.

    ☐ The writer put sentences in an order that makes sense.

C. **How do you think the writer could make the summary better?**

_____

_____

Writer's Companion • UNIT 2
Lesson 3 *More About Topic Sentence and Details*

See the rubric on page 207 for another way to evaluate the Student Model.

© Harcourt

LESSON 3: MORE ABOUT TOPIC SENTENCE AND DETAILS

Name _____

Revising the Student Model

Revise by Deleting

One thing the writer could have done better is to delete details and words that are not important. Here is an example of how the Student Model can be improved.

Example It must have been so scary.

unimportant idea _____

A. The example above is an opinion and is not an important idea in the summary. Decide which sentences are important for the summary. Write *important idea* or *unimportant idea* on the line and explain why.

1. Tortoises don't mind the spines of a cactus.

_____

_____

2. She had to move out of the animal's way before it bumped right into her!

_____

_____

3. There was just a camera between them.

_____

_____

B. Now revise the summary you wrote on page 52. Delete unimportant details or those that do not support the topic. Do your writing on another sheet of paper.

© Harcourt

Writer's Companion ▪ UNIT 2
Lesson 3 *More About Topic Sentence and Details*

LESSON 4: REVIEW ORGANIZATION

Name _____

Writer's Craft in Literature

Review Organization

An effective paragraph has a **topic sentence** that tells the main idea. It has **details** that support the main idea. Effective paragraphs often use **time-order words** to show the **sequence** in which events happen.

A. Read the paragraph about dinosaur fossils. The topic sentence is in the middle of the paragraph. It is underlined for you.

Literature Model

It took two years for a museum team to strip rock from the bones. Team members also made models to replace some of the missing bones, using what they know from other dinosaur skeletons. Almost 90% of Sue's skeleton was found, which makes it the most complete *T. rex* skeleton today. Since the first discovery in 1900, twenty-two *T. rex* skeletons have been found. Only seven of those are more than half complete.

—from *Sue, the Tyrannosaurus Rex*
by Andrew Keown

B. Review main idea, details, and time-order words.
1. Put [ ] around an important detail about Sue.
2. Put a box around the sentence that contains a time-order word or phrase. Circle the time-order word or phrase.

C. How were the missing bones replaced?

_____

_____

_____

Writer's Companion • UNIT 2
Lesson 4 *Review Organization*

56

© Harcourt

LESSON 4: REVIEW ORGANIZATION

Name _____

A Closer Look at Writer's Craft

Review Organization

In this unit, you learned that an effective paragraph contains a topic sentence and details. Most topic sentences come at the beginning of a paragraph. Some, like the one below, are at the end. Others are even in the middle.

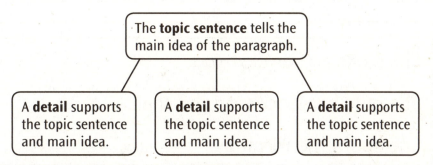

A. Read this paragraph from *Sue, the Tyrannosaurus Rex*. Notice the topic sentence and the details that support it.

> On a hot summer day in 1990, a woman named Sue Hendrickson was working with a team of fossil hunters near Faith, South Dakota. While some of the team went into a nearby town, Hendrickson stayed behind to look for fossils. What she found that day would be one of the greatest fossil discoveries ever made.

B. Use the paragraph to answer the questions below.
1. Underline the topic sentence of the paragraph.
2. Circle the main idea part of the topic sentence.
3. Box a detail sentence.

C. What happened *while* the fossil hunters went to a nearby town?

_____

_____

_____

LESSON 4: REVIEW ORGANIZATION

Name _____

Practice with Writer's Craft

Review Organization

Before you write, you should organize your ideas. Here is how one third grader organized his ideas for a how-to essay.

Idea for the topic sentence: Fiona has to clean her room.	
Order	**Steps of the Task**
1	She picks up her clothing.
3	She puts her books on the shelf.
2	She dusts the furniture.
Conclusion: Now her guests will see what a nice room she has.	

A. Read the following topic sentence in bold type. Think of what you could do to turn it into an effective paragraph.

Today, Fiona will clean her room.

1. Put the steps of the task in the correct order. Use time-order words to show the sequence.

_____

_____

_____

2. What is the main idea of the paragraph?

_____

B. Write two other details that could be added to the paragraph. Use time-order words to put them in the correct sequence.

_____

_____

_____

Writer's Companion • UNIT 2
Lesson 4 *Review Organization*

58

© Harcourt

LESSON 4: REVIEW ORGANIZATION

Name _____

Focus on the Writing Form

The Parts of a How-to Essay

A **how-to essay** usually begins with a topic sentence about what is being explained. The writer then gives the steps, using time-order words that show the sequence to follow. Here is a draft of a how-to essay written by a third grader. As you read, think about how the student organized the essay. Then answer the questions.

DRAFT

How to Play Island
by Marc

Here is how to play the game, Island. You need:

a CD player
lively music
9 sheets of colored paper
10 players

First, scatter the colored sheets of paper on the floor around the room. These are the "islands." Have someone start and stop the music. When the music starts, the players walk around the room. This is the fun part. When the music stops, each player jumps on an island. The player who is not on an island is "out." Remove an island. Then start the music again. Continue until there are two players and one island left. The last person standing on the island is the winner!

Introduce the essay with a topic sentence. It should describe the process you are explaining.

List the materials needed for the process.

Provide the steps in the order they should be done.

Use time order-words to show sequence.

Conclude by describing the result or outcome of the process.

1. Underline the sentence that tells what will be explained.
2. What materials are needed to play this game? Draw a box around them.
3. What time-order words show the sequence that should be followed?

_____

Writer's Grammar
When you list materials, you can number them or put bullets (big dots) next to them. Go back and put a number or bullet next to each item on the material list in the Student Model.

LESSON 4: REVIEW ORGANIZATION

Name _____

Evaluating the Student Model

Evaluate a How-to Essay

A. Two students were asked to write a how-to essay about something they know. This how-to essay got a score of 4. When using a 4-point rubric, a score of 4 means "excellent." Read the how-to essay and the teacher comments that go with it. Find out why this how-to essay is a success.

Student Model

How To Put Together a Jigsaw Puzzle
by Justin

Here's how I do a jigsaw puzzle. Before I start, I study the picture on the box. I spread out all the puzzle pieces on the floor, picture side up. Begin with the borders, because border pieces have a flat edge. After the borders, I look for any picture detail that stands out. Like if there's a haystack, I find all the pieces that could be a haystack. If there's a sun I look for all the pieces that could be a sun. Next, I go back to the border. If there are any weird shapes sticking out, I try to match those first. The background comes last, because it's the hardest to do. Sometimes it is just a blue sky. When that happens I take all the blue pieces and try to fit them together.

I work on three or four areas of the puzzle at the same time. When I have most of a puzzle done I look at the pieces and try to fit them in somewhere. Soon it starts to look like the picture on the box!

> Good, you introduced the topic in the first sentence.

> Nice work! You included good details that help explain the task.

> Yes! You used time-order words like *next* to show the correct order of the steps.

> You have described the result of the process and made it seem like fun too! Good job!

Writer's Companion • UNIT 2
Lesson 4 *Review Organization*

60

© Harcourt

LESSON 4: REVIEW ORGANIZATION

Name _____

Evaluating the Student Model

B. This paragraph got a score of 2. Why did it get a low score?

Can you introduce the subject in the first sentence?

Put the events in the correct order. This step should go first.

Nice use of time-order words.

We need to know the amounts of each ingredient.

This detail seems unnecessary. Can you write a better ending?

> ### Student Model
>
> **Peanut Butter Spaghetti**
> **by Philip**
>
> I like to help my mom. Last night we made spaghetti. First, my mom made the pasta. She put it into a big bowl while it was still hot. But before she did that, I made the sauce. I put some tomato paste into a big bowl and added a little water and mixed it up for a long time. You have to keep on adding water a little at a time because peanut butter is hard to mix. Finally, I add spices. I like it spicy.

C. What score would you give the student's story? Put a number on each line.

	4	3	2	1
Introduction (Topic Sentence) _____	☐ The writer states the main idea in the topic sentence.	☐ The writer gives some idea of the topic.	☐ The writer only states the topic in the title.	☐ The writer does not state the topic.
Body (Details) _____	☐ The writer tells about many of the steps to follow.	☐ The writer tells about some of the steps to follow.	☐ The writer tells about few of the steps to follow.	☐ The writer does not tell about the steps to follow.
Time-order Words _____	☐ The writer uses many time-order words.	☐ The writer uses some time-order words.	☐ The writer uses few time-order words.	☐ The writer uses no time-order words.

© Harcourt

Writer's Companion • UNIT 2
Lesson 4 *Review Organization*

LESSON 4: REVIEW ORGANIZATION

Name _____

Extended Writing/Test Prep

Extended Writing/Test Prep

On the last two pages of this lesson, you will use what you have learned
about effective paragraphs to write a longer written work.

A. **Read the three choices below. Put a star by the writing activity you would like to do.**

1. Respond to a Writing Prompt

    Writing Situation: You have to explain to a friend how to make your favorite
    sandwich.

    Directions for Writing: Think about your favorite kind of sandwich. Now write a
    how-to essay that will explain how to make it. Use what you have learned about
    topic sentences, details, and time-order words.

2. Choose one of the pieces of writing you started in this unit:
    - directions (page 40)
    - a paragraph of information (page 46)
    - a summary (page 52)

    Expand your beginning into a complete piece of writing. Use what you have learned
    in your writing.

3. Choose a topic you would like to write about. You may explain how to do an activity
    you know.

B. **Use the space below and on the next page to plan your writing.**

TOPIC: _____

_____

WRITING FORM: _____

HOW WILL I ORGANIZE MY WRITING: _____

_____

_____

_____

_____

Writer's Companion • UNIT 2
Lesson 4 *Review Organization*

62

© Harcourt

LESSON 4: REVIEW ORGANIZATION

Name _____

Extended Writing/Test Prep

C. In the space below, draw a graphic organizer that will help you plan your writing. Fill in the graphic organizer. Use the lines below to write any notes you have.

Notes

_____

_____

_____

_____

_____

_____

_____

D. Do your writing on another sheet of paper.

© Harcourt

63

Writer's Companion • UNIT 2
Lesson 4 *Review Organization*

LESSON 5: WRITING TEST PRACTICE

Name _____

Writing Test Practice

Answering Multiple-Choice Questions

Some writing tests have questions with answer choices. This lesson will help you practice this kind of test.

A. Some test questions may ask you about sentences. Read the test tip. Then read each question. Fill in the circle next to your answer.

Read the questions below. Answer questions.

1. In which sentence below is all **punctuation** correct?
   - Ⓐ I like broccoli but I don't like beets.
   - Ⓑ I like broccoli, but I don't like beets.
   - Ⓒ I like broccoli, but I don't like beets?

2. In which sentence below is all **capitalization** correct?
   - Ⓕ I have a cat named Buster.
   - Ⓖ I have a cat named buster.
   - Ⓗ I have a Cat named Buster.

3. In which sentence below is all **punctuation** correct?
   - Ⓐ We saw geese and chickens.
   - Ⓑ We saw geese, and chickens.
   - Ⓒ We saw geese and chickens?

4. In which sentence below is all **capitalization** correct?
   - Ⓕ susan and her brother are very much alike.
   - Ⓖ Susan and her brother are very much alike.
   - Ⓗ Susan and her Brother are very much alike.

Test Tip: Compound sentences are joined with a comma and a conjunction such as *and* or *but*.

Writer's Companion • UNIT 2
Lesson 5 *Writing Test Practice*

LESSON 5: WRITING TEST PRACTICE

Name _____

Writing Test Practice

B. Some tests may ask you to read a passage and answer questions about it. The sentences in the passage may be numbered. Read the test tip. Then answer the questions.

Directions: Read the passage below. Then read questions 1–4 and mark the correct answers on your Answer Sheet.

(1) There are twenty child in my class. (2) My best friend's name is Marianna. (3) Sometimes we do homework together. (4) She has two parrot. (5) One parrot's name is Polly, and there is another parrot whose name is Cracker.

1. What change, if any, should be made in sentence 1?

- A   Change *child* to **childs**
- B   Change *child* to **children**
- C   Change *class* to **classes**
- D   Make no change

> **Test Tip:**
> A compound sentence can be broken into two complete sentences.

2. Which, if any, is the correct way to revise sentence 2?

- F   My best friend's name is marianna.
- G   My best friends name is Marianna.
- H   My best friend's names is Marianna.
- J   No change is needed.

3. Which, if any, is the correct way to revise sentence 4?

- A   She has two parrots.
- B   She has two parrotes.
- C   She has two parrottes.
- D   No change is needed.

4. Which would make sentence 5 the **BEST** compound sentence?

- F   One parrot's name is Polly, or the other is Cracker.
- G   One parrot's name is Polly and the other is Cracker.
- H   One parrot's name is Polly, and the other parrot's name is Cracker.
- J   One parrot's name is Polly and the other parrot's name is Cracker.

Answer all test questions on this Answer Sheet.
1. (A) (B) (C) (D)   3. (A) (B) (C) (D)
2. (F) (G) (H) (J)   4. (F) (G) (H) (J)

Writer's Companion • UNIT 2
Lesson 5 *Writing Test Practice*

LESSON 5: WRITING TEST PRACTICE

Name _____

Writing Test Practice

C. Some test questions may ask you the best way to revise or correct sentences in a paragraph. Read the test tip. Then answer the questions on the Answer Sheet.

The following is a paragraph that may contain errors.

My Favorite Day

(1) My favorite day of the week is saturday. (2) That is when I go to the market with my dad. (3) we go there every saturday morning. (4) We get there early. (5) The farmer's are already there. (6) I would like to be a farmer someday. (7) It must be hard work!

1. Which underlined word is *not* written correctly?

A My favorite

B saturday

C my dad

D We get there early.

2. Which is the correct way to capitalize sentence 3?

F We go there every saturday morning.

G We go there every Saturday Morning.

H we go there every Saturday morning.

J We go there every Saturday morning.

3. How should the underlined words in sentence 5 be correctly written?

A The farmers

B The farmers's

C The farmers'

D Leave as is.

> **Test Tip:**
> To answer question 3, remember that a word that shows ownership contains 's or s'.

Answer all test questions on this Answer Sheet.

1. Ⓐ Ⓑ Ⓒ Ⓓ   3. Ⓐ Ⓑ Ⓒ Ⓓ

2. Ⓕ Ⓖ Ⓗ Ⓙ

Writer's Companion • UNIT 2
Lesson 5 *Writing Test Practice*

LESSON 5: WRITING TEST PRACTICE

Name _____

Writing Test Practice

D. **Some test questions may ask you about parts of sentences.**
Read the test tip. Then answer the questions.

Read the paragraph. Read each question and mark the circle next to the correct answer.

Yesterday our class went to the zoo in __(1)__. First, we saw the seals. We saw them eat their lunch. Two __(2)__ fed them. The seals did tricks. After lunch they took a nap, __(3)__ we went to see the birds. One __(4)__ feathers were all white.

1. Which answer should go in blank (1)?

Ⓐ jacksonville

Ⓑ Jacksonville

Ⓒ zoo

2. Which answer should go in blank (2)?

Ⓕ woman

Ⓖ womans

Ⓗ women

3. Which answer should go in blank (3)?

Ⓐ or

Ⓑ so

Ⓒ unless

4. Which answer should go in blank (4)?

Ⓕ birds

Ⓖ bird's

Ⓗ birds'

> **Test Tip:**
> When more than one person or thing owns something else, it is shown with an *s'*. For instance, *pigs'* in *the pigs' tails*, tells us that there is more than one pig and each pig has a tail.

© Harcourt

Writer's Companion ▪ UNIT 2
Lesson 5 *Writing Test Practice*

LESSON 1: SUPPORTING AN OPINION

Name _____

Writer's Craft in Literature

Look at Supporting an Opinion

Sometimes when you write, you will express an **opinion**. An opinion tells how you feel or what you think about something.

A. Read the following passage from *The Stories Julian Tells*. Notice how Julian feels about friends who are girls and about Huey's friend.

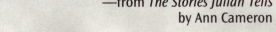

> If you have a girl for a friend, people find out and tease you. That's why I didn't want a girl for a friend — not until this summer, when I met Gloria.
>
> It happened one afternoon when I was walking down the street by myself. My mother was visiting a friend of hers, and Huey was visiting a friend of his. Huey's friend is five and so I think he is too young to play with.

—from *The Stories Julian Tells* by Ann Cameron

B. Identify details from the passage that show opinions.
  1. Underline Julian's opinion in the first paragraph.
  2. Circle Julian's opinion in the second paragraph.

C. Write the words that tell why Julian feels the way he does.

_____

_____

Writer's Companion • UNIT 3
Lesson 1 *Supporting an Opinion*

LESSON 1: SUPPORTING AN OPINION

Name _____

A Closer Look at Writer's Craft

Explore Supporting an Opinion

You can support your opinions by giving **reasons** or **details**.

A. Read each sentence. Circle whether each is an opinion or a supporting detail.

Example Winter is the best time of year.
DETAIL   (OPINION)

1. The swimming pool is five miles away.
   DETAIL   OPINION

2. Going to the movies is really fun.
   DETAIL   OPINION

3. The woods are scary at night.
   DETAIL   OPINION

B. Read the paragraph. Think about the opinion. Underline the reasons that support the opinion.

   People should keep their dogs on leashes in the park. There is a leash law, but people don't follow it. A dog off the leash can be a danger. It can bite someone or knock a child down. It can also get in fights with other dogs.

C. Think of another reason that supports the opinion. Write it on the lines.

_____

_____

Writer's Companion • UNIT 3
Lesson 1 *Supporting an Opinion*

LESSON 1: SUPPORTING AN OPINION

Name _____

Practice with Writer's Craft

Use Supporting an Opinion

To persuade means to get someone to do something or to think in a certain way. Here is how one third grader planned a paragraph that persuades.

Example My Opinion: _My dog is the best pet in the world._

Reason 1	Reason 2	Reason 3
He is always ready to play.	He listens when I tell him my problems.	He guards the house.

A. What kind of animal do you think makes the best pet? Write your opinion on the line. Then complete the chart with reasons that persuade.

My Opinion: _____

Reason 1	Reason 2	Reason 3

B. Use information from your chart to write a paragraph that states and supports your opinion. Do your writing on another sheet of paper.

Writer's Companion • UNIT 3
Lesson 1 *Supporting an Opinion*

© Harcourt

LESSON 1: SUPPORTING AN OPINION

Name _____

Focus on the Writing Form

The Parts of a Persuasive Paragraph

A **persuasive paragraph** uses reasons and details to support a strong **opinion.** Below is an example of a persuasive paragraph written by a third grader. As you read, think about how the student supported her opinion. Then answer the questions.

Student Model

DRAFT

My Favorite Pet
by Marci

Gully is my dog, and he is the best pet in the world. He is great at listening. All day and all night, he guards the house. No matter what is bothering me, he makes me feel better. I always feel safe with him. He is always ready to play, so I never get bored. He is also very smart, much smarter than my friends' dogs. He'll play with a ball, a toy, or even a sock. He obeys many different commands.

Introduce the opinion in a clear topic sentence.

Organize the reasons and details in an order that makes sense.

Develop the argument in sentences that present your reasons.

Conclude by restating the opinion or calling for action.

1. Which sentence states an opinion? Underline it.
2. Which sentences give reasons? Put boxes around them.
3. Which sentences seem to be out of order? Circle them. Then draw an arrow to the place where you think each sentence belongs.

Writer's Grammar
In a plural possessive noun, the apostrophe comes last. For example: *Students' books* or *dogs' bones.* Find plural possessive nouns in the Student Model.

LESSON 1: SUPPORTING AN OPINION

Name _____

Evaluating the Student Model

Evaluate a Persuasive Paragraph

When you evaluate a persuasive paragraph, ask yourself these questions:

- Does the writer express a strong opinion?
  (Look for signal words such as *think, believe, feel, best,* and *worst.*)

- Does the writer place reasons in a logical order?
  (Look for an order that makes sense.)

A. Reread the Student Model on page 71. Then answer these questions.

1. How does the writer feel about her dog?

   _____

2. Name two reasons why the writer feels that way.

   _____

   _____

B. Now evaluate the Student Model. Put a check in the box next to each thing the writer has done well. If you do not think the writer did a good job with something, do not check the box.

- ☐ The writer introduced the opinion in a strong topic sentence.
- ☐ The reasons and details are in a logical order.
- ☐ The writer included at least three reasons.
- ☐ The writer concluded by restating the opinion or calling for action.

C. How do you think the writer could make the persuasive paragraph better? Write your ideas below.

_____

_____

_____

Writer's Companion • UNIT 3
Lesson 1 *Supporting an Opinion*

See the rubric on page 207 for another way to evaluate the Student Model.

© Harcourt

LESSON 1: SUPPORTING AN OPINION

Name _____

Revising the Student Model

Revise by Rearranging Sentences

When you revise a persuasive paragraph, you want to put your reasons in a logical order. Sometimes, this means that you need to move, or rearrange, your sentences. Here is an example of how a part of the Student Model can be improved.

Example The sentence *He is great at listening* should be moved close to *He obeys many different commands.*

A. Revise these groups of sentences from the Student Model. Put them in an order that makes more sense to you.

1. All day and all night, he guards the house. No matter what is bothering me, he makes me feel better. I always feel safe with him.

_____

_____

_____

_____

2. He is always ready to play, so I never get bored. He is also very smart, much smarter than my friends' dogs. He'll play with a ball, a toy, or even a sock.

_____

_____

_____

_____

B. Revise the paragraph you wrote on page 70. Focus on writing a clear opinion with reasons and details that support your opinion. Rearrange your sentences so they make the most sense. Do your writing on another sheet of paper.

© Harcourt

73

Writer's Companion • UNIT 3
Lesson 1 *Supporting an Opinion*

LESSON 2: STAYING ON TOPIC

Name _____

Writer's Craft in Literature

Look at Staying on Topic

When you write, it is important to **stay on topic**. To do this, you must make sure all the sentences in a passage are about the topic of the passage.

A. Read the following passage. Notice how the writer's sentences tell about the topic.

> **Literature Model**
>
> On Friday our class put on the best talent show in the whole world. For his talent, Boomer Fenton showed his birthmark in the shape of a dog's face. Kelsey played "Twinkle, Twinkle, Little Star" on her violin. Leo tried to get his dog to roll over, but the dog ran under Ms. Babbitt's chair and wouldn't come out for the rest of the show. Carol Ann and Wendy did the bee poem. Carol Ann's crown fell off right in the middle of it.
>
> —from *The Talent Show* by Susan Wojciechowski

B. Decide if the sentences are on or off the topic.
  1. Circle the sentence that tells the topic.
  2. Underline the sentences that are about the topic.
  3. Choose which one of the sentences below is off the topic of the passage. Put a box around it.

   Linda sang a song in a very high voice.
   Doug went on a trip to Oregon with his father.

C. Reread the passage above. What is the author's opinion about the talent show.

_____

_____

Writer's Companion • UNIT 3
Lesson 2 *Staying on Topic*

LESSON 2: STAYING ON TOPIC

Name _____

A Closer Look at Writer's Craft

Explore Staying on Topic

To stay on topic, your sentences all need to support your topic.

> **Staying on Topic**
>
> The **topic sentence** states the main idea.   **Detail sentences** suppport the topic sentence.

A. Read the sentences below. Think about which ones are on topic and which ones are not. Cross off the sentence in each group that is not on topic.

Example Tomás decided to bake a pie. He got out the sugar, the butter, and the flour. ~~He watched a show on television.~~

1. Rob really wanted to get on the baseball team. He was taller than the other boys in his class. He practiced batting and catching until he was tired.

2. My brother is the kindest person I know. He always helps around the house. He helps anyone in trouble. He gets very good grades.

B. Read the paragraph. Think about the topic. Cross out the sentence that is not on topic.

> The storm raced across the prairie. The sky got darker and darker. The fields were turning green. The wind began to blow. Suddenly, the clouds opened, and rain poured down.

C. Write another detail sentence that could tell about the storm.

_____

_____

_____

© Harcourt

75

Writer's Companion • UNIT 3
Lesson 2 *Staying on Topic*

LESSON 2: STAYING ON TOPIC

Name _____

Practice with Writer's Craft

Use Staying on Topic

Speeches are often written to persuade people to believe or to do something. When you plan a speech that persuades, start with a topic sentence that states your opinion. Then list some details about your topic. Here is how one student planned a speech about doing yoga.

Example

Topic Sentence	Yoga is a great activity that everyone should try.
Details	Yoga is relaxing Helps you get stronger Stretches muscles Good for every age group

A. Think about something you like to do and want to persuade others to do. Write a topic sentence. Write details that tell about your topic.

Topic Sentence	
Details	

B. Use information from your chart to write a speech that persuades. Remember to stay on topic. Do your writing on another sheet of paper.

Writer's Companion • UNIT 3
Lesson 2 *Staying on Topic*

76

© Harcourt

LESSON 2: STAYING ON TOPIC

Name _____

Focus on the Writing Form

The Parts of a Speech

A good **speech** tries to persuade the audience to believe something or to do something. Below is a draft written by a third grader. As you read, think about how the student organized it. Then answer the questions.

Student Model

DRAFT

A Perfect Activity
by Maria

Yoga is a great activity that everyone should try. Part of each yoga class is spent just thinking and breathing. It can really relax you. You might be worried about something at the start of a yoga class. By the end, you will feel calm. Yoga can help you get stronger. Other sports help you get stronger, too. It is a good way to stretch your whole body. It works every muscle you have. Even your face and your feet will feel stretched. People of every age can take yoga. There are classes for seniors, and there are classes for kids.

Get the audience's attention with a strong statement of your opinion.

State reasons that support your opinion.

Add details that will appeal to your audience. Be sure the details are on topic. Put them in a logical order.

Conclude by restating your opinion and calling your listener to action.

1. Which sentence states the topic? Underline it.
2. Find one sentence that tells more about the topic. Put a box around it.
3. Circle one sentence that seems to be out of order. Then draw an arrow to the place where you think this sentence belongs.
4. Which sentence is not on topic? Cross it out.

© Harcourt

Writer's Grammar
An action verb describes an action (*Crystal **runs** fast.*) and a linking verb connects the subject to information about the subject (*The kite **is** red.*). The Student Model contains both kinds of verbs. Find some action verbs or linking verbs.

77

Writer's Companion • UNIT 3
Lesson 2 *Staying on Topic*

LESSON 2: STAYING ON TOPIC

Evaluating the Student Model

Name _____

Evaluate a Speech

When you evaluate a speech, ask yourself these questions:

- Does the writer get the audience's attention?
  (Look for a strong opinion statement.)

- Does the writer state reasons in a logical order?
  (Look for an order that makes sense.)

- Does the writer stay on topic?
  (Look for details that support the opinion.)

A. Reread the Student Model on page 77. Then answer these questions.

1. What is the writer's opinion? _____

   _____

2. What reasons does the writer give? _____

   _____

B. Now evaluate the Student Model. Put a check in the box next to each thing the writer has done well. If you do not think the writer did a good job with something, do not check the box.

- ☐ The writer began with a strong opinion statement.
- ☐ The writer used reasons and details to support the opinion.
- ☐ The writer put reasons and details in a logical order.
- ☐ The detail sentences are on topic.
- ☐ The writer concluded by restating the opinion or calling for action.

C. How do you think the writer could make the speech better? Write your ideas below.

_____

_____

_____

© Harcourt

Writer's Companion • UNIT 3
Lesson 2 *Staying on Topic*

78

See the rubric on page 207 for another way to evaluate the Student Model.

LESSON 2: STAYING ON TOPIC

Name _____

Revising the Student Model

Revise by Rearranging Sentences

When you revise a speech, make sure the reasons and details are in a logical order. Put the most persuasive reason at the end of the speech. Here is an example of how a group of sentences from the Student Model can be rearranged. Think about which order is more effective.

Example Yoga is a great activity that everyone should try. Part of each yoga class is spent just thinking and breathing. It can really relax you.

Revised: Yoga is a great activity that everyone should try. It can really relax you. Part of each yoga class is spent just thinking and breathing.

A. Revise each group of sentences from the Student Model. Change the order. Then put a star next to the order you think works best.

1. Yoga can help you get stronger. It is a good way to stretch your whole body. It works every muscle you have.

_____

_____

_____

2. It is a good way to stretch your whole body. It works every muscle you have. Even your face and your feet will feel stretched.

_____

_____

_____

B. Revise the speech you wrote on page 76. Rearrange your sentences in a logical order. Put the most persuasive reason at the end. Do your writing on another sheet of paper.

© Harcourt

79

Writer's Companion ▪ UNIT 3
Lesson 2 *Staying on Topic*

LESSON 3: REASONS AND EXAMPLES

Name _____

Writer's Craft in Literature

Look at Reasons and Examples

When writers want readers to agree with their opinions, they support those opinions with reasons and examples. A **reason** tells why something is true. An **example** shows that it is true.

A. Read the following conversation between José and his father, Mr. Mendez. Notice how José's father supports his opinion.

Literature Model

"And one more thing. Forget about trying to hit like I did, okay? You don't have to. You're a born outfielder, José! You've made catches that I never would have been able to, not in a million years."

José stared at him. "Really? You mean you... don't mind that I can't hit?"

José's father chuckled. "Can't hit'? If you call belting a grand slam homer not hitting, well, son, we've got to sit down and have a serious talk about the game of baseball! José, you're a born ballhawk, so stop worrying about the hitting and concentrate on your fielding. That's where your team needs you the most."

—from *Centerfield Ballhawk*
by Matt Christopher

B. Find the reasons and examples that support José's father's opinion.
1. Circle the sentence that states José's father's opinion.
2. Underline one reason that supports the opinion.
3. Put an X by one example that supports the opinion.

C. What is Mr. Mendez's opinion of José's playing? Write it in your own words.

_____

Writer's Companion • UNIT 3
Lesson 3 *Reasons and Examples*

LESSON 3: REASONS AND EXAMPLES

Name _____

A Closer Look at Writer's Craft

Explore Reasons and Examples

When you write an opinion, you can support it with **reasons** and **examples**.

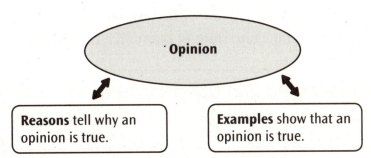

A. Read each short passage below. Circle the word that tells if it contains a REASON or an EXAMPLE.

Example Living on a farm is great. You get to take care of all kinds of farm animals.

(REASON)   EXAMPLE

1. My sister is a wonderful singer. Last year she won a statewide singing contest.

    REASON   EXAMPLE

2. Marco is a good friend. I can tell him anything, and he will always listen.

    REASON   EXAMPLE

B. Read the passage below. Underline the reason. Circle the example.

   My dog is the smartest dog around. He can understand and obey all my commands. When I tell him to count to five, he raises his paw five times.

C. Add another example to the passage above.

_____

_____

_____

81

Writer's Companion • UNIT 3
Lesson 3 *Reasons and Examples*

LESSON 3: REASONS AND EXAMPLES

Name _____

Practice with Writer's Craft

Use Reasons and Examples

A persuasive letter states an opinion and supports it with reasons and examples. It tries to persuade readers to do or think something. When you plan a persuasive letter, write your opinion. Then list reasons and examples that support it. Here is how one student planned a persuasive letter.

Example My Opinion: _Lin should join the debate team._

Reasons	Examples
We need a good teammate. Lin speaks well in public. Lin is good at doing research.	Our team has lost four of our last five debates. Everyone loved her speech on recycling. She got an A on our last research report.

A. Think of a friend whom you would like to join a club, team, or activity. Write your opinion. Then list reasons and examples to support your opinion.

My Opinion: _____

Reasons	Examples

B. Use information from your chart to write a persuasive letter to your friend. Include at least two reasons and one example. Do your writing on another sheet of paper.

Writer's Companion • UNIT 3
Lesson 3 *Reasons and Examples*

LESSON 3: REASONS AND EXAMPLES

Name _____

Focus on the Writing Form

The Parts of a Persuasive Letter

Below is an example of a **persuasive letter** written by a third grader. As you read, think about how the writer organized the letter. Then answer the questions.

Student Model

DRAFT

97 North Dover Rd.
Afton, MI 49705
October 4, 2006

Dear Lin,

I'm writing to you because I think you would be a great member of our debate team. You speak really well. I saw you give the speech on recycling last month. You were great! You are also good at telling jokes.

We need you to make our team stronger. Our team has lost four of our last five debates. We need a good speaker to make us a better team.

You are also good at doing research. You got an A on the last research report. You said you liked doing it. Our team really needs you!

Your friend,
Sam

> **Introduce the topic** by writing the heading and the greeting. Write an opening sentence that states your opinion clearly.

> **State three reasons** in a logical order.

> **Develop** your reasons by giving examples.

> **Conclude** by restating your opinion and calling for action.

> **Finish** with a closing and your signature.

1. Which sentence states the writer's opinion? Underline it.
2. What is the strongest reason the writer gives? Put a box around it.
3. Circle one example the writer gives.
4. Which sentence is not supported by reasons and examples? Put an X next to it.

Writer's Grammar
All abbreviations, except for the postal abbreviations of states, need a period at the end. Find a postal abbreviation in the letter.

83

Writer's Companion • UNIT 3
Lesson 3 *Reasons and Examples*

LESSON 3: REASONS AND EXAMPLES

Name _____

Evaluating the Student Model

Evaluate a Persuasive Letter

When you evaluate a persuasive letter, ask yourself these questions:

- Does the writer begin with a strong opinion?
  (Look for words that tell what the writer feels or thinks.)

- Does the writer give reasons in a logical order?
  (Look for the strongest reason at the end of the letter.)

- Does the writer support the opinion with examples?
  (Look for words that show that the opinion is true.)

A. Reread the Student Model on page 83. Then answer these questions.

    1. What is the writer's opinion?

    _____

    2. What reasons does the writer give?

    _____

B. Now evaluate the Student Model. Put a check in the box next to each thing the writer has done well. If you do not think the writer did a good job with something, do not check the box.

☐ The writer began with a strong opinion.
☐ The writer supported the opinion with reasons that tell why the opinion is true.
☐ The writer used examples that show why the opinion is true.
☐ The writer put reasons from least important to most important.
☐ The writer ended by restating the opinion and calling for action.

C. How do you think the writer could make the end of the letter better? Write your ideas below.

_____

_____

Writer's Companion • UNIT 3
Lesson 3 *Reasons and Examples*

84

See the rubric on page 207 for another way to evaluate the Student Model.

© Harcourt

LESSON 3: REASONS AND EXAMPLES

Name _____

Revising the Student Model

Revise by Rearranging Reasons

When you revise a persuasive letter, you should start with the weakest reason and move to the strongest reason. One thing the writer could have done better is rearrange his reasons from weakest to strongest.

A. Rearrange the body of the Student Model. Change the order of the reasons from weakest to strongest. Use the Word Bank to help you.

I'm writing to you because I think you would be a great member of our debate team. You speak really well. I saw you give the speech on recycling last month. You were great! You are also good at telling jokes.

We need you to make our team stronger. Our team has lost four of our last five debates. We need a good speaker to make us a better team.

You are also good at doing research. You got an A on the last research report. You said you liked doing it.

Word Bank

first
next
most important
_____
_____
_____
_____

_____

_____

_____

_____

_____

_____

_____

B. Revise the letter you wrote on page 82. Put the reasons in order from weakest to strongest. Write your letter on a separate sheet of paper.

Writer's Companion • UNIT 3
Lesson 3 *Reasons and Examples*

LESSON 4: REVIEW IDEAS

Name _____

Writer's Craft in Literature

Review Ideas

When you write an opinion, you should support it with reasons and examples. Your details should all stay on topic.

A. Below is a passage from *Ramona Forever*. As you read it, think about Ramona's opinion.

Literature Model

Ramona sat back and buckled her seat belt. She had once looked like Roberta. Amazing! She had once been that tiny, but she had grown, her hair had calmed down when she remembered to comb it, and she had learned to use her eyes and hands. "You know what I think?" she asked, and did not wait for an answer. "I think it is hard work to be a baby."

—from *Ramona Forever*
by Beverly Cleary

B. Reread the passage to find the opinion and reasons that support it.
1. Underline Ramona's opinion.
2. Circle the reasons Ramona gives.

C. Write a new example that supports Ramona's opinion.

_____

_____

Writer's Companion • UNIT 3
Lesson 4 *Review Ideas*

86

LESSON 4: REVIEW IDEAS

Name _____

A Closer Look at Writer's Craft

Review Ideas

Writers often express opinions. Then they give reasons and examples to support these opinions.

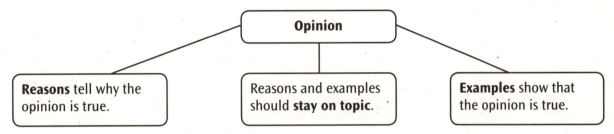

A. Read the beginning of this article. Look for reasons and examples that support the opinion.

> It is important to be prepared for a fire at home. Floods can also be dangerous. If you and your family have a fire safety plan, you will be safer in a fire. The Pérez family's house burned down last month. They followed their fire safety plan. No one was hurt. A fire safety plan can also help firefighters.

B. Write the information.

Example Write a reason: _If you and your family have a fire safety plan, you will be safer in a fire._

1. Write an opinion: _____

2. Write a reason: _____

3. Write an example: _____

C. Write the sentence that is not on topic.

_____

87

Writer's Companion • UNIT 3
Lesson 4 *Review Ideas*

LESSON 4: REVIEW IDEAS

Name _____

Practice with Writer's Craft

Review Ideas

When you plan a review of a book, you decide if you like the book or not. Then you give reasons and examples for your opinion. Read the example in the box below. It shows how a third grader began to think about a book review.

My Opinion of *Ramona Forever*: I loved the book.
Reason 1: Ramona is a funny character.
Reason 2: Ramona feels the way I do about many things.
Reason 3: Ramona learns from her mistakes.

A. **1. How does the writer feel about *Ramona Forever*?**

_____

_____

2. Which of the reasons would be most important to you? Explain why.

_____

_____

B. Write a new example to support one of the reasons from the chart. Tell which reason you are supporting.

_____

_____

_____

_____

_____

Writer's Companion • UNIT 3
Lesson 4 *Review Ideas*

LESSON 4: REVIEW IDEAS

Name _____

Focus on the Writing Form

The Parts of a Review

In this unit, you have learned how writers develop their work when they write an opinion. Below is a first draft of a review written by a third grader. As you read, think about how the student organized the review. Then answer the questions.

Student Model

DRAFT

Ramona Forever
by Gina

I loved the book *Ramona Forever* by Beverly Cleary. It is the story of Ramona Quimby and her family. She has a sister, Beezus. Her mother is about to have a baby. Ramona isn't too happy about the baby. She has always been the baby of the family. She is afraid the baby will take her place. Babies are often troublesome.

Ramona feels the way I do about many things. She has mixed-up feelings about her family and friends. She has a terrible argument with her sister. Just like a real person.

Ramona is a funny character. She is always making mistakes and getting in trouble. Still, she learns from her mistakes.

I thought *Ramona Forever* was a wonderful book about a real-life girl.

> **Introduce** the review by stating your opinion.

> **Support** your opinion with reasons and examples.

> **Provide** details that are on topic.

> **End** by restating your opinion and calling readers to action.

1. Underline the sentence that tells an opinion.
2. Underline a reason that supports the opinion.
3. Draw a box around an example that tells about the reason.

Writer's Grammar
Remind students that a pronoun takes the place of a noun. Explain that a subject pronoun is one that can be used as the subject of a sentence: *I, you, he, she, it, we,* and *they* are subject pronouns. Find a subject pronoun in the Student Model.

Writer's Companion • UNIT 3
Lesson 4 *Review Ideas*

LESSON 4: REVIEW IDEAS

Name _____

Evaluating the Student Model

Evaluate a Review

A. Two students were asked to write a review. The review below got a score of 4. When using a 4-point rubric, a score of 4 means "excellent." Read the review and the teacher comments that go with it. Find out why this is a success.

Student Model

DRAFT

The Saturdays
by Veronica

The Saturdays by Elizabeth Enright is an amazing book that is really fun to read. It is the story of the four Melendy children, Mona, Rush, Randy, and Oliver. One rainy Saturday, they are very bored. Randy has a great idea. They will form a club, the Saturdays. They will put all their allowance money together. Each Saturday, one of them will take all the money and have an adventure.

Randy goes first because the club was her idea. She goes to the ballet. There she meets Mrs. Oliphant. She is an old friend of the family. Mrs. Oliphant takes Randy to tea and tells her thrilling stories of her own childhood.

Mona goes next. She gets her long, long hair chopped off. Then Rush goes to the opera. He loves music, so the opera is very special to him. Last, it is Oliver's turn. He is only six, so he is not allowed to go out by himself. He sneaks out anyway and goes to the circus. Then he gets lost. A policeman brings him home on a horse.

The author makes these characters come alive. I felt like I knew them all. Their adventures are exciting to read about. I wished I could go along. You'll find that reading about the Melendys' adventures is almost as much fun as having them yourself!

> Good – you state your opinion strongly here.

> These examples are very nice!

> Good word choice.

> You use different sentence structures here to keep the review interesting.

> You give some excellent reasons to read the book.

> Nice – you restate your opinion and call your readers to action!

© Harcourt

Writer's Companion • UNIT 3
Lesson 4 *Review Ideas*

90

LESSON 4: REVIEW IDEAS

Name _____

Evaluating the Student Model

B. This paragraph got a score of 2. Why did it get a low score?

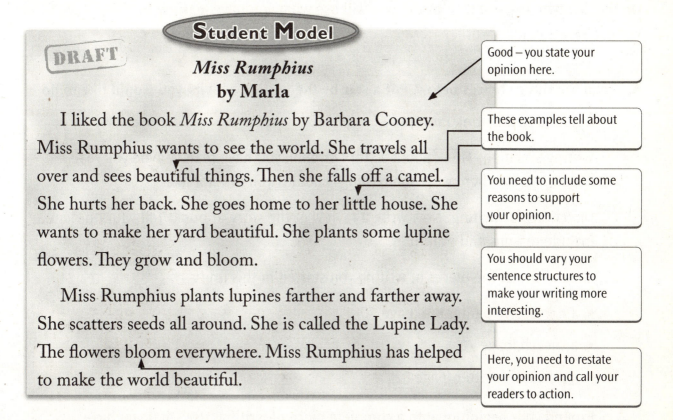

Student Model

DRAFT

Miss Rumphius
by Marla

I liked the book *Miss Rumphius* by Barbara Cooney. Miss Rumphius wants to see the world. She travels all over and sees beautiful things. Then she falls off a camel. She hurts her back. She goes home to her little house. She wants to make her yard beautiful. She plants some lupine flowers. They grow and bloom.

Miss Rumphius plants lupines farther and farther away. She scatters seeds all around. She is called the Lupine Lady. The flowers bloom everywhere. Miss Rumphius has helped to make the world beautiful.

- Good — you state your opinion here.
- These examples tell about the book.
- You need to include some reasons to support your opinion.
- You should vary your sentence structures to make your writing more interesting.
- Here, you need to restate your opinion and call your readers to action.

C. What score would you give the student's story? Put a number on each line.

	4	3	2	1
Ideas ____	☐ Writer gives a strong opinion with reasons and examples.	☐ Writer gives an opinion with some reasons or examples.	☐ Writer only gives an opinion.	☐ Writer does not give an opinion, reasons, or examples.
Words and Sentences ____	☐ Writer uses vivid words and details. Sentences vary.	☐ Writer uses some vivid details and varied sentences.	☐ Writer uses few vivid details. Sentences do not vary.	☐ Writer uses unclear words. Sentences do not vary.
Organization ____	☐ Student presents information in logical, interesting sequence, which audience can follow.	☐ Student presents information in logical, sequence, which audience can follow.	☐ Audience has difficulty following presentation because student jumps around.	☐ Audience cannot understand presentation because there is no sequence of information.

LESSON 4: REVIEW IDEAS

Name _____

Extended Writing/Test Prep

Extended Writing/Test Prep

On the last two pages of this lesson, you will use what you have learned to write a longer written work.

A. **Read the three choices below. Put a star by the writing activity you would like to do.**

1. Respond to a Writing Prompt

   Writing Situation: Think about a story or book you have read. Maybe you really liked it. Maybe there were some things about it you did not like.

   Directions for Writing: Now write a review of the story or book. Tell your opinion. Include reasons and examples.

2. Choose one of the pieces of writing you started in this unit:

   • a persuasive paragraph (page 70)

   • a speech (page 76)

   • a persuasive letter (page 82)

   Expand your beginning into a complete piece of writing. Use what you have learned about writing opinions.

3. Choose a topic you would like to write about. You may write a persuasive paragraph, a speech, or a persuasive letter. Use reasons and examples to support your opinion.

B. **Use the space below and on the next page to plan your writing.**

TOPIC: _____

WRITING FORM: _____

HOW WILL I ORGANIZE MY WRITING: _____

_____

_____

Writer's Companion • UNIT 3
Lesson 4 *Review Ideas*

92

LESSON 4: REVIEW IDEAS

Name _____

Extended Writing/Test Prep

C. In the space below, draw a graphic organizer that will help you plan your writing. Fill in the graphic organizer. Write additional notes on the lines below.

Notes

_____

_____

_____

_____

_____

_____

_____

_____

D. Write your paragraph, speech, or letter on another sheet of paper.

© Harcourt

93

Writer's Companion ▪ UNIT 3
Lesson 4 *Review Ideas*

LESSON 5: WRITING TEST PRACTICE

Name _____

Writing Test Practice

Answering Multiple-Choice Questions

This lesson will help you answer different kinds of multiple-choice questions often found in writing tests. Read each question. Mark your answer on the Answer Sheet.

A. For some multiple-choice questions, you will have to read three or four sentences and decide which sentence is written correctly. Read the test tip. Then practice answering this type of test question.

1. Which sentence below is correct?

   A   The girls' bikes were piled in a heap.

   B   The girls bikes were piled in a heap.

   C   The girls bikes' were piled in a heap.

2. In which sentence below is all **capitalization** correct?

   F   I opened my mouth so Dr. parsons could look inside.

   G   I opened my mouth so Dr. Parsons could look inside.

   H   I opened my mouth so dr. Parsons could look inside.

> **Test Tip:**
> To make a plural noun possessive, add an apostrophe (') after the *s*. (Example: my friends' jackets.)

3. Which sentence below is correct?

   A   The cars horns all honked at once.

   B   The cars horns' all honked at once.

   C   The cars' horns all honked at once.

4. Which sentence below is correct?

   F   Mr. and Mrs. Sami live next door.

   G   Mr. and mrs. sami live next door.

   H   Mr and Mrs Sami live next door.

© Harcourt

Answer all test questions on this Answer Sheet.

1. Ⓐ   Ⓑ   Ⓒ   3. Ⓐ   Ⓑ   Ⓒ

2. Ⓕ   Ⓖ   Ⓗ   4. Ⓕ   Ⓖ   Ⓗ

Writer's Companion ▪ UNIT 3
Lesson 5 *Writing Test Practice*

LESSON 5: WRITING TEST PRACTICE

Name _____

Writing Test Practice

B. For some multiple-choice questions, you will have to read a passage and then decide the best way to revise or correct a sentence. Read the test tip. Then practice answering this kind of question.

DIRECTIONS

Read the introduction and the passage that follows. Then read each question and fill in the circle next to the correct answer.

Cilla is in the third grade. She wrote this personal narrative. She wants you to help her revise and edit the narrative. Read Cilla's narrative and think about the changes she should make. Then answer the questions that follow.

The Flood

(1) It was the fourth rainy day in a row. (2) The river behind the house was too full. (3) It just kept raining. (4) I and my brothers were worried. (5) Mom and Dad rushed we into the car. (6) We came back three days later. (7) My brothers shouts told us what happened. (8) The river had come into our house. (9) There was mud in every room!

1. What is the **BEST** way to revise sentence 4?
   - (A) I and my brothers was worried.
   - (B) My brothers and I were worried.
   - (C) I and my brothers were worry.
   - (D) No revision is needed.

2. What change, if any, should be made in sentence 5?
   - (F) Change *we* to **us**
   - (G) Change *Dad* to **dad**
   - (H) Change *rushed* to **rushing**
   - (J) Make no change

3. What change, if any, should be made in sentence 7?
   - (A) Change *shouts* to **shouted**
   - (B) Change *my* to **me**
   - (C) Change *brothers* to **brothers'**
   - (D) Make no change

> **Test Tip:**
> When listing people in a personal narrative, list yourself last.
>
> INCORRECT:
> I and he went outside.
>
> CORRECT:
> He and I went outside.

© Harcourt

95

Writer's Companion • UNIT 3
Lesson 5 *Writing Test Practice*

LESSON 5: WRITING TEST PRACTICE

Name _____

Writing Test Practice

C. For some writing tests, you will have to answer questions based on a graphic organizer. Samara made the plan to organize ideas for a paper. Use her plan to answer questions 1 and 2 on the Answer Sheet.

Story/Movie/Show: Mr. Popper's Penguins	Audience: My classmates
Opinion: Mr. Popper's Penguins is a great book.	

| Reason 1: I love to read. |
| Details: |
| Reason 2: The action in the story is very exciting. |
| Details: Mr. Popper is in a car chase to get ice for his penguins. |
| Reason 3: |
| Details: Waddling penguins are so cute. |
| Opinion Restated/Action Requested: You should read this book! |

1. Based on the information in Samara's Writing Plan, what kind of paper is she planning to write?

    A   a story
    B   a review
    C   a how-to essay
    D   a journal/diary entry

2. Which statement below is off topic and should be taken out of Samara's Writing Plan?

    F   *Mr. Popper's Penguins* is a great book.
    G   The action in the story is very exciting.
    H   I love to read.
    I   You should read this book!

Test Tip: To decide if a statement is off topic, ask yourself what it tells you about the topic of a particular piece of writing. If it does not add information, it is off topic.

Answer all test questions on this Answer Sheet.

1.   2.

Writer's Companion • UNIT 3
Lesson 5 Writing Test Practice

LESSON 5: WRITING TEST PRACTICE

Name _____

Writing Test Practice

D. For some multiple-choice questions, you will choose which sentence or group of words is written correctly. Read the test tip. Read each question and mark your answer on the Answer Sheet.

1. Which sentence is written correctly?

A   The girls was so mad that they could hardly talk.

B   The girl was so mad that she could hardly talk.

C   The girl was so mad that her could hardly talk.

D   The girl was so mad that them could hardly talk.

2. Which sentence is written correctly?

A   The singers' voices were clear and high.

B   The singers voices' were clear and high.

C   The singer's voice's were clear and high.

D   The singer's voices were clear and high.

3. Which address is written correctly?

A   2041 South Millburn ave.
Carmel, CA. 90041

B   2041 South Millburn Ave
Carmel, ca 90041

C   2041 South Millburn Ave.
Carmel, CA 90041

D   2041 South Millburn ave
Carmel, ca 90041

Test Tip:
All postal abbreviations are written in full capital letters.

© Harcourt

Answer all test questions on this Answer Sheet.

1. Ⓐ   Ⓑ   Ⓒ   Ⓓ   3. Ⓐ   Ⓑ   Ⓒ   Ⓓ

2. Ⓐ   Ⓑ   Ⓒ   Ⓓ

97

Writer's Companion • UNIT 3
Lesson 5 *Writing Test Practice*

LESSON 1: COMBINING SENTENCES

Name _____

Writer's Craft in Literature

Look at Combining Sentences

Short, choppy sentences often make writing uninteresting to read. By **combining** subjects, predicates, and whole sentences, your writing will become more interesting and easier to understand. Use the **conjunctions** *and* or *but* when you combine parts of sentences or whole sentences.

A. Read the following model. Notice how the writer uses conjunctions to combine sentences.

Literature Model

"You're right, Chita! The snake was brown and round and as long as this living room. It raised up its head, squinted its beady eyes, and squinched toward us. But Majestic reared his front legs and zigzagged through the field, while I waved my sword and shouted strong words. We confused that snake, and it snake-snaked away in another direction."

—from *Papa Tells Chita a Story* by Elizabeth Fitzgerald Howard

B. Identify the combined sentences.
1. Underline sentences that might have been combined.
2. Circle one or more conjunctions in each sentence you underlined.

C. Choose one of the sentences you underlined. On the lines below, write two short sentences that might have been combined.

_____

_____

_____

Writer's Companion • UNIT 4
Lesson 1 *Combining Sentences*

98

LESSON 1: COMBINING SENTENCES

Name _____

A Closer Look at Writer's Craft

Explore Combining Sentences

Combine short sentences with *and* or *but* to make longer, smoother sentences.

Short Sentences		Combined Sentences
• Suzi likes tacos. Bret likes tacos. • Suzi likes pizza. Bret likes subs. • Suzi eats pizza. Suzi drinks milk.	and or but	• Suzi *and* Bret like tacos. • Suzi likes pizza, *but* Bret likes subs. • Suzi eats pizza *and* drinks milk.

A. Use a conjunction to combine each pair of sentences. Write the combined sentences on the lines.

1. Sonia has skates. Robert has skates.

   _____

2. Lucas saw smoke. Lucas called for help.

   _____

3. Roni wants to go to the movies. Roni must do her homework.

   _____

   _____

B. Read this combined sentence from *Papa Tells Chita a Story*. Write three smaller sentences that might have been combined to make the longer sentence.

   But now Papa is resting and reading and waiting for Chita.

1. _____

2. _____

3. _____

99

Writer's Companion • UNIT 4
Lesson 1 *Combining Sentences*

LESSON 1: COMBINING SENTENCES

Name _____

Practice with Writer's Craft

Use Combining Sentences

Before you compare any two things or people, think about how they are alike. Combining your sentences can help you compare. Words like *both*, *alike*, and *similar*, as well as conjunctions, can help you combine subjects, predicates, and sentences. Here is how one student started to think about comparing two of her friends.

Things about Janey	Things about Jessie	Things about Both
Janey is smart.	Jessie is smart.	Janey and Jessie are both smart.
Janey wears jeans and T-shirts.	Jessie wears jeans and T-shirts.	They dress alike in jeans and T-shirts.
Janey plays piano.	Jessie plays flute.	Janey and Jessie are musicians.
Janey loves to read.	Jessie writes stories and poems.	Janey and Jessie like language arts.

A. Think about two people you know. Write their names on the lines. Then complete the chart.

Things about _____	Things about _____	Things about Both

B. Use information from your chart to write a short paragraph comparing two people. Use another sheet of paper.

Writer's Companion ▪ UNIT 4
Lesson 1 *Combining Sentences*

LESSON 1: COMBINING SENTENCES

Name _____

Focus on the Writing Form

The Parts of a Paragraph that Compares

A **paragraph that compares** begins with a topic sentence. The other sentences give examples and details that support the topic. Below is a draft by a third grader. As you read, look for examples and details that compare the two people.

Student Model

DRAFT

My Two Best Friends
by Samantha

My two best friends Janey and Jessie are a lot alike. People get them mixed up. First of all, they look alike. Janey and Jessie have straight dark hair. Janey and Jessie have bangs. They also dress alike. Janey and Jessie wear the same kind of jeans. They wear they same kind of sneakers. They are both smart. Also, they have similar interests. Janey likes to read, but Jessie writes stories and poems. They both like music. Janey plays piano. Jessie plays flute. Also, Janey's name starts with a J. Jessie's name starts with a J. They are my best friends in the whole entire world.

> **Begin** with a topic sentence that tells what two things are being compared.

> **Give** examples of how the two things are alike.

> **Add** interesting details to support the examples.

> **Conclude** by restating your main point.

---

1. Which sentence introduces the topic? Underline it.
2. How are Janey and Jessie alike? Find examples. Put boxes around them.
3. Circle *both, alike,* and *similar* in the Student Model.
4. Write the following sentence as two shorter sentences.

    Janey likes to read, but Jessie writes stories and poems.

Writer's Grammar

Janey is a subject. *Jessie* is a subject. When you combine sentences, the subject and the verb must agree. Remember to change the verb when you combine subjects: (Janey *is* my best friend. Janey and Jessie *are* my best friends.).

Writer's Companion • UNIT 4
Lesson 1 *Combining Sentences*

LESSON 1: COMBINING SENTENCES

Evaluating the Student Model

Name _____

Evaluate a Paragraph that Compares

When you evaluate a paragraph that compares, ask yourself these questions:

- Does the writer clearly state the two things that are being compared?
  (Look for a topic sentence that tells what two things are being compared.)

- Does the writer provide several examples of how the two things are alike?
  (Look for examples of how the things are alike.)

A. Reread the Student Model on page 101. Then follow the directions below.

   1. Write two more examples of how Janey and Jessie are alike.

   _____

   _____

   2. Write a detail that tells something similar, but not exactly alike about the girls.

   _____

   _____

B. Now evaluate the Student Model. Check the box next to each thing the writer has done well. If you do not think the writer did a good job with something, do not check the box.

- ☐ The topic sentence clearly states what two things are being compared.
- ☐ The writer gave several examples.
- ☐ The writer gave interesting details to support the examples.
- ☐ The writer used comparison words such as *both, alike,* and *similar.*
- ☐ The writer combined sentences to make them more interesting.
- ☐ The writer concluded by restating the main point.

C. How do you think the writer could make the paragraph better? Write your ideas below.

_____

_____

Writer's Companion • UNIT 4
Lesson 1 *Combining Sentences*

102

See the rubric on page 207 for another way to evaluate the Student Model.

© Harcourt

LESSON 1: COMBINING SENTENCES

Name _____

Revising the Student Model

Revise by Making Sentences Clearer

The student writer could have made the sentences clearer by combining sentences or sentence parts. Here is an example of how a sentence from the Student Model can be improved.

Example   Also, Janey's name starts with a J. Jessie's name starts with a J.

Also, both names start with the letter J.

A. Revise these sentences from the Student Model. Improve the sentences by combining subjects, predicates, or whole sentences.

1. Janey and Jessie have straight dark hair. Janey and Jessie have bangs.

_____

2. Janey plays piano. Jessie plays flute.

_____

3. Janey and Jessie wear the same kind of jeans. They wear they same kind of sneakers.

_____

B. Revise the paragraph you wrote on page 100. Combine sentences where necessary to make your writing clearer and easier to understand. Use another sheet of paper, if necessary.

_____

_____

_____

_____

_____

_____

© Harcourt

Writer's Companion • UNIT 4
Lesson 1 *Combining Sentences*

LESSON 2: SENTENCE VARIETY

Name _____

Writer's Craft in Literature

Look at Sentence Variety

When your sentences are varied, your writing becomes more interesting to read. One way to **vary sentences is by length**. Another way is by using **different kinds of sentences**. Three kinds of sentences and their end marks are: **statements** (.), **exclamations** (!), and **questions** (?).

A. Read the Literature Model. Notice how the writer uses statements, exclamations, and questions.

Literature Model

One summer night, as he was relaxing in the cool grass with his friend Bear, Coyote had an idea. "I think I will climb to the heavens and discover their secrets!"

Bear scratched his big head and asked, "How can you do that?"

"I can get up there with no trouble at all," Coyote said.

—from *Coyote Places the Stars*
retold by Harriet Peck Taylor

B. Identify the different kinds of sentences.
1. Underline a statement.
2. Draw a box around an exclamation.
3. Circle a question that either Bear or Coyote asks.

C. Rewrite a sentence from the Literature Model as another kind of sentence.

_____

_____

_____

Writer's Companion • UNIT 4
Lesson 2 *Sentence Variety*

104

LESSON 2: SENTENCE VARIETY

A Closer Look at Writer's Craft

Name _____

Explore Sentence Variety

When you change an end mark, the meaning of your sentence can change, too. Say each sentence below to yourself. Notice the extra expression added to the bolded word or words in each sentence.

Statement	Question	Exclamation
I did that.	I did **that**?	I **did** that!

A. Rewrite each sentence to vary it. Change words and end mark.

1. I have a toy poodle.

_____

_____

2. I have a very nice dog.

_____

_____

B. Read this sentence from *Coyote Places the Stars*. Notice the sentence type.

"I think I will climb to the heavens and discover their secrets!"

C. What would you say to coyote about this plan?

1. Write a question.

_____

2. Write a statement.

_____

3. Write an exclamation.

_____

© Harcourt

Writer's Companion • UNIT 4
Lesson 2 *Sentence Variety*

LESSON 2: SENTENCE VARIETY

Name _____

Practice with Writer's Craft

Use Sentence Variety

Before you write a paragraph that contrasts, think about how your subjects are different. You should also plan to vary your sentences when you write. Here is how one student started to plan a paragraph that contrasts his two grandmothers.

Example **Question about** *My Grandmothers:* How are they different?

Exclamation about *Grandma Bernice: She has a horse!*

Exclamation about *Grandma Melanie: Her hair is tomato red!*

Statement about *Grandma Bernice: Grandma Bernice is a vet, but she likes to sew, too.*

Statement about *Grandma Melanie: Grandma Melanie is tall and thin.*

A. Think about two things or two people who are different from each other. Use varied kinds of sentences to plan writing about them.

Question about _____ **: How are they different?**

Exclamation about _____ : _____
               Name 1

Exclamation about _____ : _____
               Name 2

Statement about _____ : _____
            Name 1

_____

Statement about _____ : _____
            Name 2

_____

B. Use your sentences to write a short paragraph about how the two things or two people are different. Write your paragraph on another sheet of paper.

Writer's Companion • UNIT 4
Lesson 2 *Sentence Variety*

106

© Harcourt

LESSON 2: SENTENCE VARIETY

Name _____

Focus on the Writing Form

The Parts of a Paragraph that Contrasts

A **paragraph that contrasts** tells how things or people are different. It begins with a topic sentence that clearly states what is being contrasted. Below is a draft by a third grader. As you read, think about how the student organized the paragraph.

DRAFT

Different Grandmas
by Ethan

I have two grandmas. They are very different. One is Grandma Bernice, and one is Grandma Melanie. Grandma Melanie is tall and thin. Grandma Bernice is short and round. Grandma Melanie has long hair in a braid. Her hair is tomato red! Grandma Bernice's hair is gray and curly. Another thing that is different is where they live. Grandma Melanie lives in the city. She lives nearby in a big building. Grandma Bernice lives far away. She lives on a farm. They have different jobs, too. Grandma Melanie is a teacher. She teaches reading and writing. Grandma Bernice is a vet, but she likes to sew, too. Do you know what else? She has a horse! The horse is named Horace. My two grandmas are different. I love them the same.

Introduce two subjects to contrast.

Organize your ideas. Provide three examples for each thing you contrast.

Develop ideas by adding details about color, shape, and size.

Conclude by restating your main point.

1. Which sentences introduce the topic? Underline them.
2. Write three details, contrasting the grandmothers. _____
_____
_____

3. Circle the concluding sentences.

Writer's Grammar
Many adjectives appeal to the senses: *sight, sound, touch, taste,* and *smell*. In the sentence, *Grandma Melanie is tall and thin,* the words *tall* and *thin* are adjectives that appeal to the sense of sight. Find other adjectives in the Student Model.

107

Writer's Companion • UNIT 4
Lesson 2 *Sentence Variety*

LESSON 2: SENTENCE VARIETY

Name _____

Evaluating the Student Model

Evaluate a Paragraph that Contrasts

When you evaluate a paragraph that contrasts, ask yourself these questions:

- Does the writer introduce two subjects to contrast?
  (Look for a topic sentence.)

- Does the writer provide three examples?
  (Look for sentences that tell how the subjects are different.)

- Does the writer use varied sentence types?
  (Look for different end marks and conjunctions.)

A. Reread the Student Model on page 107. Then answer these questions.

 1. Write two examples that contrast the way the grandmas look.

_____

_____

 2. Write two details that appeal to the senses.

_____

B. Now evaluate the Student Model. Check the box next to each thing the writer has done well. If you do not think the writer did a good job with something, do not check the box.

- ☐ The writer included a topic sentence that tells what is being contrasted.
- ☐ The writer described differences using three examples.
- ☐ The writer gave interesting details to support the examples.
- ☐ The writer used different kinds of sentences.
- ☐ The writer concluded by restating the main point.

C. How do you think the writer could make the paragraph of contrast better? Write your ideas below.

_____

_____

Writer's Companion • UNIT 4
Lesson 2 *Sentence Variety*

108

See the rubric on page 207 for another way to evaluate the Student Model.

© Harcourt

LESSON 2: SENTENCE VARIETY

Name _____

Revising the Student Model

Revise by Making Contrasts Clearer

The student writer should make the contrasts clearer and easier to understand. One way to do this is by combining sentences. Here is an example of how a sentence from the Student Model can be improved.

Example I have two grandmas. They are very different.

I have two grandmas who are very different.

A. Read each pair of sentences from the Student Model. Combine the pair into one sentence.

1. Grandma Melanie is tall and thin. Grandma Bernice is short and round.

_____

_____

2. My two grandmas are different. I love them the same.

_____

_____

B. Revise the paragraph you wrote on page 106. Combine and vary your sentences. Use another sheet of paper, if necessary.

_____

_____

_____

_____

_____

_____

© Harcourt

Writer's Companion • UNIT 4
Lesson 2 *Sentence Variety*

LESSON 3: MORE ABOUT SENTENCE VARIETY

Name _____

Writer's Craft in Literature

Look at More About Sentence Variety

Writers use a mix of long sentences and short sentences. They use statements, exclamations, and questions. **Sentence variety** makes writing more interesting.

A. Read the model. Notice how the writer uses a variety of sentences.

Literature Model

The big snake raised his head and said, "Good morning, Iguana."

The iguana did not answer but limbered on, bobbing his head, badamin, badamin.

"Now why won't he speak to me?" said the python to himself. "Iguana must be angry about something. I'm afraid he is plotting some mischief against me!"

—from *Why Mosquitoes Buzz in People's Ears*
retold by Verna Aardema

B. Identify different kinds of sentences.
  1. Underline the conjunctions.
  2. Draw a box around an exclamation.
  3. Circle a question the python asks.

C. Which two sentences can be combined into one? Combine them below. Use proper punctuation and end marks.

_____

_____

_____

Writer's Companion • UNIT 4
Lesson 3 *More About Sentence Variety*

110

LESSON 3: MORE ABOUT SENTENCE VARIETY

Name _____

A Closer Look at Writer's Craft

Explore More About Sentence Variety

Sentence variety makes writing more interesting.

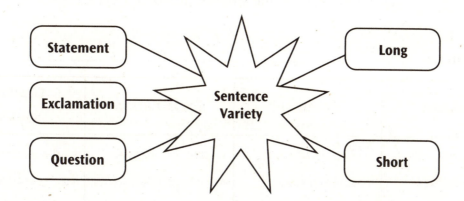

A. Draw a line from the sentence to the word that describes it. Then write the correct end mark on the line.

combined	1. The corn grew very tall last summer ____
exclamation	2. Do you know my sister ____
question	3. Our friend is moving away, and we will miss him ____
short	4. Your hat is huge ____
statement	5. Squirrels scampered ____

B. Read the combined sentence from *The Ant and the Grasshopper*. Underline the conjunction. On the lines, rewrite the sentence as two or three separate sentences.

Winter arrived a week later and brought whirls of snow and ice.

1. _____

2. _____

3. _____

C. Rewrite one of the short sentences about winter as a different kind of sentence.

_____

111

Writer's Companion • UNIT 4
Lesson 3 *More About Sentence Variety*

LESSON 3: MORE ABOUT SENTENCE VARIETY

Name _____

Practice with Writer's Craft

Use More About Sentence Variety

Before you write a paragraph that explains, think about the topic and details you want to include. Here is how one student planned a paragraph about leaves.

Example **Topic:** _Leaves_

Question	Statement	Exclamation	Combined Sentence
Have you ever noticed that some leaves change color at different parts of the year?	This happens every year.	This is how trees get ready for winter!	The leaves can be yellow, red, or purple.

A. Think about something you would like to explain. Write your main idea. Then fill out the rest of the chart.

Topic: _____

Question	Statement	Exclamation	Combined Sentence

B. Use information from your chart to write a short paragraph that explains. Use another sheet of paper.

Writer's Companion • UNIT 4
Lesson 3 *More About Sentence Variety*

LESSON 3: MORE ABOUT SENTENCE VARIETY

Name _____

Focus on the Writing Form

The Parts of a Paragraph that Explains

The purpose of a **paragraph that explains** is to tell about something.
The paragraph starts with a topic sentence that gives the main idea. The
supporting sentences give details and information. Below is a draft by a
third grader. As you read, think about the parts of the paragraph and the
varied sentences.

Student Model

DRAFT

Leaves
by Jenny Sue

Have you ever noticed that some leaves change color
at different parts of the year? This is how trees get ready
for winter! Sometimes the leaves look green. At the end of
summer, some trees stop feeding their leaves. This is how
the other colors come out. The leaves can be yellow or red.
The leaves can be purple, too. Leaves turn red if they have a
lot of sugar in them. Then, some trees lose their leaves. This
happens every year.

> **Begin** with a sentence that clearly introduces your topic.

> **Add** facts, examples, and details.

> Put your ideas in an **order** that makes sense.

> **Conclude** by restating your main idea.

1. What is the writer's purpose for writing this paragraph?

_____

2. Which sentence introduces the topic? Underline it.
3. Double underline a fact and detail that supports the fact.
4. Which two short sentences could be combined into a longer one? Combine them below.

_____

5. Put a box around the concluding sentence.

© Harcourt

Writer's Grammar
Too and *also* have the same meaning. Put a comma (,) before *too* when it's the last word in the
sentence. Find *too* in the Student Model.

113

Writer's Companion • UNIT 4
Lesson 3 *More About Sentence Variety*

LESSON 3: MORE ABOUT SENTENCE VARIETY

Name _____

Evaluating the Student Model

Evaluate a Paragraph that Explains

When you evaluate a paragraph that explains, ask yourself these questions:

- Does the writer clearly state the main idea?
  (Look for a topic sentence that tells what is being explained.)

- Does the writer provide facts and details that explain the main idea?
  (Look for examples and interesting details.)

A. Reread the Student Model on page 113. Then answer these questions.

1. Write a sentence that tells something about leaves. _____

_____

2. Write two details that support the idea that leaves change color to get ready for

winter. _____

_____

B. Evaluate the Student Model. Put a check in the box next to each thing the writer has done well. If you do not think the writer did a good job, do not check the box.

- ☐ The writer included a topic sentence that clearly states what is being explained.
- ☐ The writer provided facts and examples to support the main idea.
- ☐ The writer used different kinds of sentences.
- ☐ The writer concluded by restating the main idea.

C. How do you think the writer could make the paragraph better? Write your ideas below.

_____

_____

_____

_____

Writer's Companion • UNIT 4
Lesson 3 *More About Sentence Variety*

114

See the rubric on page 207 for another way to evaluate the Student Model.

© Harcourt

LESSON 3: MORE ABOUT SENTENCE VARIETY

Name _____

Revising the Student Model

Revise by Adding Details

One way the writer can make the paragraph more interesting is by adding details. Here is how a sentence from the Student Model can be improved.

Example Sometimes the leaves look green.

In the spring and summer, the leaves look green.

A. Revise these sentences from the Student Model. Make the sentences clearer and more detailed. Use words from the Word Bank.

1. This is how the other colors come out.

_____

2. Then, some trees lose their leaves.

_____

3. This happens every year.

_____

_____

> **Word Bank**
> fresh
> hidden underneath
> in the winter
> new
> pretty
> springtime
> _____
> _____
> _____
> _____

B. Revise the paragraph you wrote on page 112. Add some interesting details. Remember to vary and combine your sentences. Use another sheet of paper, if you need more space.

_____

_____

_____

_____

_____

_____

© Harcourt

115

Writer's Companion • UNIT 4
Lesson 3 *More About Sentence Variety*

LESSON 4: REVIEW SENTENCE FLUENCY

Name _____

Writer's Craft in Literature

Review Sentence Fluency

Good writers vary their sentences to make their writing interesting. They use statements, exclamations, and questions. They use short sentences and longer, combined sentences.

A. Below are sentences from a story about three sisters who outsmart a wolf. Notice the sentence variety as you read.

Literature Model

But an old wolf lived nearby and saw the good mother leave. At dusk, disguised as an old woman, he came up to the house of the children and knocked on the door twice: bang, bang.

Shang, who was the eldest, said through the latched door, "Who is it?"

"My little jewels," said the wolf, "this is your grandmother, your Po Po."

"Po Po!" Shang said. "Our mother has gone to visit you!"

—from *Lon Po Po* retold by Ed Young

B. Review sentence variety.
  1. Underline a statement.
  2. Put a box around a question asked by a character.
  3. Circle an exclamation.

C. Choose a longer, combined sentence from the model. Write the two short sentences that the longer sentence might have come from.

_____

_____

_____

LESSON 4: REVIEW SENTENCE FLUENCY

Name _____

A Closer Look at Writer's Craft

Review Sentence Fluency

In this unit, you learned about different kinds of sentences.

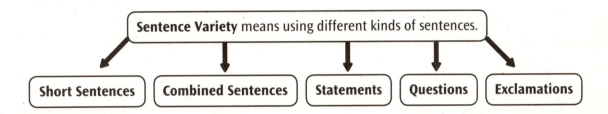

A. Read this sentence from *Lon Po Po*.

   The journey is long, my children, and the day is short.

B. Write the combined sentence as two short sentences.

   1. _____

   2. _____

C. Rewrite each of these sentences from *Lon Po Po*. Add words and variety to make the sentences more interesting.
   1. The wolf was furious.

   _____

   _____

   2. Have you eaten gingko nuts?

   _____

   _____

   3. Soon the old wolf pretended to be sleepy.

   _____

   _____

117

Writer's Companion • UNIT 4
Lesson 4 *Review Sentence Fluency*

LESSON 4: REVIEW SENTENCE FLUENCY

Name _____

Practice with Writer's Craft

Review Sentence Fluency

Before you write an essay that compares and contrasts, think about what your topic and supporting details will be. Then think about the different kinds of sentences you will use to add interest to your writing. Here is how one third grader planned an essay explaining how two folktales are alike and different.

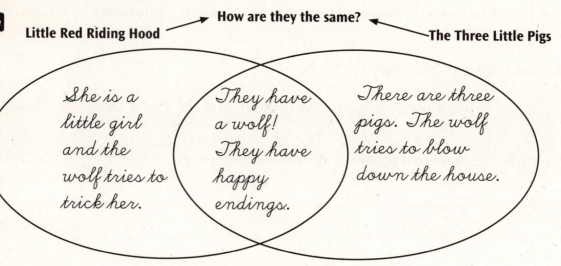

A. Answer the questions based on the writing plan.

1. Who are the main characters in *Little Red Riding Hood*? _____
   _____

2. Who are the main characters in *The Three Little Pigs*? _____
   _____

3. How are the wolves alike in both stories? _____
   _____

B. Write two sentences—one that compares and one that contrasts something from both stories.

_____

_____

_____

Writer's Companion • UNIT 4
Lesson 4 Review Sentence Fluency

LESSON 4: REVIEW SENTENCE FLUENCY

Name _____

Focus on the Writing Form

The Parts of a Compare and Contrast Essay

A **compare and contrast essay** tells how two things are alike and how they are different. Below is a draft written by a third grader. As you read, think about how the student organized the essay.

Student Model

DRAFT

Two Stories
by Leticia

Little Red Riding Hood and *The Three Little Pigs* are two stories that are alike and different. Do you want to know how they are similar? Both have a wolf in it! The wolf is bad and scares them. The wolf loses in the end and both stories have happy endings.

Here is how the stories are different. Red Riding Hood is a little girl. *The Three Little Pigs* has three pigs. The wolf tries to trick Red Riding Hood, but the wolf tries to blow down the houses of the three pigs. So that's how these two stories are alike and different.

> **Introduce** the topic and state the main idea of the essay.

> State a **main idea** of how the two things are **alike**. Give an example to support that idea.

> State a **main idea** of how the two things are **different**. Give an example to support that idea.

> **Conclude** by restating your main idea.

1. What is the topic of the essay?

_____

2. Find sentence that give examples of how the stories are **alike**. Put [ ] around it.
3. Find sentences that give examples of how the stories are **different**. Draw a box around them.
4. Circle the concluding sentence.

© Harcourt

> **Writer's Grammar**
> Remember that the article *a* changes to *an* when the noun it describes starts with a vowel. For example, "I have *a* banana, but not *an* orange." Find the use of *a* in the model.

Writer's Companion • UNIT 4
Lesson 4 *Review Sentence Fluency*

LESSON 4: REVIEW SENTENCE FLUENCY

Name _____

Evaluate the Writer's Form

Evaluate a Compare and Contrast Essay

A. Two students were asked to write an essay comparing and contrasting two folktales. This essay got a score of 4. When using a 4-point rubric, a score of 4 means "excellent." Read the compare and contrast essay and the teacher comments that go with it. Find out why it is a success.

Student Model

DRAFT

Two Stories
by Seth

The Tortoise and the Hare and *The Grasshopper and the Ants* are alike. They are also different. Both stories have animals that act like people. In both, one character works hard and one does not. The one that works hard wins!

What are the differences? In *The Grasshopper and the Ants,* they are getting ready for the winter, but in *The Tortoise and the Hare* they are having a race. In *The Grasshopper and the Ants,* the grasshopper wants to have fun, but in the other story the hare is playing a trick. So even though they are different, they teach the same lesson.

> Great! You introduced the topic in the first sentence.

> Yes! You used sentences that vary in length.

> Good! You used a variety of sentences.

> Way to go! You used examples and details to support your main points.

> Good job! You have restated the main point at the end.

© Harcourt

Writer's Companion • UNIT 4
Lesson 4 *Review Sentence Fluency*

120

LESSON 4: REVIEW SENTENCE FLUENCY

Name _____

Evaluate the Writer's Form

B. The essay below got a score of 2. When using a 4-point rubric, a score of 2 means "needs improvement." Read the essay and the teacher comments that go with it. Find out why it received a score of 2.

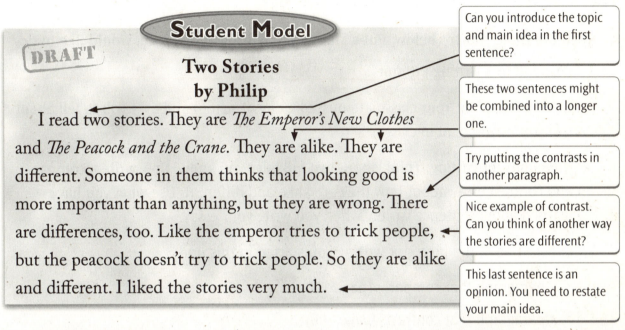

Student Model

DRAFT

Two Stories
by Philip

I read two stories. They are *The Emperor's New Clothes* and *The Peacock and the Crane.* They are alike. They are different. Someone in them thinks that looking good is more important than anything, but they are wrong. There are differences, too. Like the emperor tries to trick people, but the peacock doesn't try to trick people. So they are alike and different. I liked the stories very much.

Teacher comments:
- Can you introduce the topic and main idea in the first sentence?
- These two sentences might be combined into a longer one.
- Try putting the contrasts in another paragraph.
- Nice example of contrast. Can you think of another way the stories are different?
- This last sentence is an opinion. You need to restate your main idea.

C. This chart is an example of a 4-point rubric. A score of 4 is the highest score in this rubric. A score of 1 is the lowest score. Use the teacher comments above to complete the rubric. Write a number score on the line in the first column.

	4	3	2	1
Sentences _____	☐ The writer varies the sentences.	☐ The writer varies some of the sentences.	☐ The writer does not vary many of the sentences.	☐ The writer does not vary the sentences at all.
Development _____	☐ The essay has a clear main idea and strong details.	☐ The essay has a main idea and is supported by details.	☐ The essay does not have a clear main idea and has few supporting details.	☐ The main idea is not clear and there are few or no supporting details.
Word Choice _____	☐ The writer uses clear, exact words and phrases. The writing is interesting to read.	☐ The word choices are clear. The writer uses some interesting words and phrases.	☐ The writer does not use words or phrases that make the writing clear to the reader.	☐ The writer uses word choices that are unclear or poor.

Writer's Companion • UNIT 4
Lesson 4 *Review Sentence Fluency*

LESSON 4: REVIEW SENTENCE FLUENCY

Name _____

Extended Writing/Test Prep

Extended Writing/Test Prep

On the last two pages of this lesson, you will use what you have learned about sentence variety to write a longer written work.

A. Read the three choices below. Put a star by the writing activity you would like to do.

1. Respond to a Writing Prompt

Writing Situation: Your classmate missed a day of school and asks you to tell about two stories you read in class.

Directions for Writing: Think about two folktales you know. Now write a compare and contrast essay about how they are alike and different. Use what you have learned about sentence variety when you write your essay.

2. Choose one of the pieces of writing you started in this unit:

- a paragraph that compares (page 100)

- a paragraph that contrasts (page 106)

- a paragraph that explains (page 112)

Expand your beginning into a complete piece of writing. Use what you have learned about different kinds of sentences in your writing.

3. Choose two favorite meals or foods. Write an essay that compares and contrasts them. Use different types of sentences in your writing.

B. Use the space below and on the next page to plan your writing.

TOPIC: _____

_____

WRITING FORM: _____

HOW WILL I ORGANIZE MY WRITING: _____

_____

Writer's Companion • UNIT 4
Lesson 4 *Review Sentence Fluency*

LESSON 4: REVIEW SENTENCE FLUENCY

Name _____

Extended Writing/Test Prep

C. In the space below, draw a graphic organizer that will help you plan your writing. Fill in the graphic organizer. Use the lines below to write your notes.

Notes

_____

_____

_____

_____

_____

_____

_____

© Harcourt

D. Write your essay on another sheet of paper.

123

Writer's Companion • UNIT 4
Lesson 4 *Review Sentence Fluency*

LESSON 5: WRITING TEST PRACTICE

Name _____

Writing Test Practice

Answering Multiple-Choice Questions

Some writing tests have questions with answer choices. This lesson will
help you practice this kind of test.

A. Some test questions may ask you to put sentences in order. Read the test tip. Then
read each question. Mark the circle next to the correct answer.

1. Put the ideas in the box together to create a sentence that makes sense.

> there is a
> my jacket
> hole in
> big

Which sentence correctly combines the words from the box?

Ⓐ There is a my jacket hole in big.

Ⓑ There is a hole in big my jacket.

Ⓒ There is a big hole in my jacket.

2. Put the ideas in the box together to create a sentence that makes sense.

> apple
> brown bowl
> from the
> I took an

Which sentence correctly combines the words from the box?

Ⓕ From the apple brown bowl I took an.

Ⓖ I took an apple from the brown bowl.

Ⓗ I took an brown bowl from the apple.

Test Tip:
The article *a*
usually comes
before a word
that begins with a
consonant (*a* bear;
a pot). The word
an usually comes
before a word
that begins with
a vowel (*an* egg;
an ox).

© Harcourt

Writer's Companion • UNIT 4
Lesson 5 *Writing Test Practice*

124

LESSON 5: WRITING TEST PRACTICE

Name _____

Writing Test Practice

B. Miranda's teacher asked the students in her class to write a paragraph about a family trip. Here is a first draft of Miranda's paragraph.

Read the test tip. Then answer questions 1–3 on the Answer Sheet below.

(1) I love to go camping with my family. (2) We go to the state park. (3) It is several miles upstate. (4) Last weekend we had the most fun. (5) At night we made a big campfire. (6) We told stories that were scary.

1. In sentence 3, which is an adjective that describes *how many*?

   A It

   B is

   C several

   D upstate

2. In sentence 4, which is an adjective that compares?

   F weekend

   G had

   H the

   I most

3. In sentence 5, which is an adjective that describes *what kind*?

   A at

   B night

   C made

   D big

> **Test Tip:**
> There are many types of adjectives. Some adjectives tell *what kind* (small; red). Some adjectives tell *how many* (some; few). Some adjectives compare (older; oldest).

© Harcourt

Answer all test questions on this Answer Sheet.	
1. (A) (B) (C) (D)	3. (A) (B) (C) (D)
2. (F) (G) (H) (I)	

125

Writer's Companion • UNIT 4
Lesson 5 *Writing Test Practice*

LESSON 5: WRITING TEST PRACTICE

Name _____

Writing Test Practice

C. Read the introduction, test tip, and the passage that follows. Then read each question and fill in the correct answer on your Answer Sheet.

James is in the third grade. He wrote this report about his brothers. He wants you to help him revise and edit the report. Read James's report and think about the changes he should make.

My Big Brothers

(1) I have two brothers. (2) I am the youngest one. (3) It is fun having brothers who are oldest. (4) They teach me lots of things. (5) Justin is teaching me to play drums. (6) He is an good drummer. (7) Richie helps me with my homework. (8) He is also teaching me chess.

1. What is the **BEST** way to revise sentence 1?

   A   I have three brother.

   B   I have two brother.

   C   I have one brothers.

   D   No revision is needed.

2. What change, if any, should be made in sentence 3?

   F   Change **brothers** to **brother**

   G   Change **brothers** to **a brothers**

   H   Change **oldest** to **older**

   J   Make no change

3. What change, if any, should be made in sentence 6?

   A   Change **good** to **gooder**

   B   Change **an** to **a**

   C   Change **good** to **best**

   D   Make no change

> **Test Tip:**
> Make sure that an adjective that tells *how many* matches its noun.
> **CORRECT:** four books; one book
> **INCORRECT:** four book; one books

© Harcourt

Answer all test questions on this Answer Sheet.

1. Ⓐ   Ⓑ   Ⓒ   Ⓓ   3. Ⓐ   Ⓑ   Ⓒ   Ⓓ

2. Ⓕ   Ⓖ   Ⓗ   Ⓘ

Writer's Companion • UNIT 4
Lesson 5 *Writing Test Practice*

126

LESSON 5: WRITING TEST PRACTICE

Name _____

Writing Test Practice

D. Read "Spelling." Then read the test tip. Choose the word or words that correctly complete questions 1–4. Fill in the circle next to the correct answer.

Spelling

I am good at spelling, but my sister Jenny is ___(1)___. She has won many contests. She can spell words with many syllables. Next month she will enter ___(2)___ big contest in the city. Then she will go on to the state championship. Maybe she will be ___(3)___ famous than I will be. I help her learn ___(4)___ additional word every day.

1. Which answer should go in blank (1)?
   - Ⓐ speller
   - Ⓑ gooder
   - Ⓒ better

2. Which answer should go in blank (2)?
   - Ⓕ a
   - Ⓖ an
   - Ⓗ those

3. Which answer should go in blank (3)?
   - Ⓐ most
   - Ⓑ better
   - Ⓒ more

4. Which answer should go in blank (4)?
   - Ⓕ a
   - Ⓖ an
   - Ⓗ more

> **Test Tip:**
> When comparing two things, use a different word than when comparing more than two things.
> **two:** worse; redder
> **more than two:** worst; reddest

© Harcourt

Writer's Companion • UNIT 4
Lesson 5 *Writing Test Practice*

LESSON 1: TOPIC AND NOTES

Name _____

Writer's Craft in Literature

Look at Topic and Notes

What do you do first when you get ready to write? You choose a **topic,** which is what you will write about. You think about the **purpose,** which is the reason for writing. You also think about the **audience,** or who will read your writing. Your topic should not be longer than a few words. It guides you in doing research, taking notes, writing, and revising.

A. Read the following Literature Model. Think about the writer's topic.

> **Literature Model**
>
> The year the corn grew tall and straight, Leah's papa bought her a pony. The pony was strong and swift and sturdy, with just a snip of white at the end of his soft black nose. Papa taught Leah to place her new saddle right in the middle of his back and tighten the girth around his belly, just so.
>
> —from *Leah's Pony* by Elizabeth Friedrich

B. Read to figure out the topic.
  1. Underline the title of the book.
  2. Circle words from the title that you see in the paragraph.

C. What is the topic of the paragraph? How did the title and repeated words help you figure it out? Write your answer on the lines.

_____

_____

_____

_____

Writer's Companion • UNIT 5
Lesson 1 *Topic and Notes*

LESSON 1: TOPIC AND NOTES

Name _____

A Closer Look at Writer's Craft

Explore Topic and Notes

You can start thinking about your topic with a very big idea. Then you can narrow the idea a little bit. Then you can narrow it more. Then you'll have your topic!

A. Read the information in each triangle. Then circle the topic that belongs on the line.

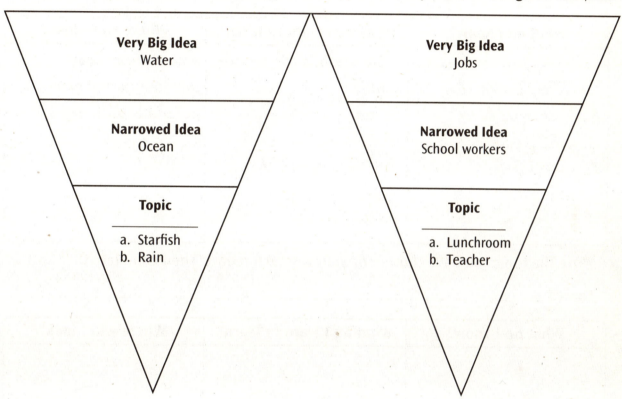

B. Read the very big idea and the narrowed idea. Then write a possible topic.

Very Big idea: Seasons   Narrowed idea: Winter   Topic: _____

C. Prepare to write a research report. Write a very big idea that interests you. Then write a narrowed idea. Finally, write the topic for your research report.

Very big idea: _____

Narrowed idea: _____

Topic: _____

129

Writer's Companion • UNIT 5
Lesson 1 *Topic and Notes*

LESSON 1: TOPIC AND NOTES

Name _____

Practice with Writer's Craft

Use Topic and Notes

What do you do after you choose the topic? You prepare to take careful notes. This chart shows how one third grader used important questions to prepare.

Example Topic: _How Ants Work and Live_

What do I know?	What do I want to learn?	Where will I look?
1. Ants live in hills. 2. They build the hills themselves. 3. They can carry heavy things.	1. How do ants work together? 2. How do they get their food? 3. Why don't they drown in their hills when it rains?	encyclopedias nature magazines science Web sites

A. Write the topic you have chosen for your research report. Then complete the chart.

Topic: _____

What do I know?	What do I want to learn?	Where will I look?

B. Use another sheet of paper. Write each of the questions from the "What do I want to learn?" part of your chart. Tell where you will look for answers to each of the questions. Use information from the "Where will I look?" part of your chart to help you.

Writer's Companion • UNIT 5
Lesson 1 Topic and Notes

© Harcourt

LESSON 1: TOPIC AND NOTES

Name _____

Focus on the Writing Form

The Parts of Notes

Careful **notes** tell where you found your information. They tell more about the topic. They include only facts, not opinions. The boxes below show an article and the notes a third grader took while reading the article. Read the article and then take notes. Then answer the questions.

How Do Ants Live?

We talked to a local scientist who studies ants. She said they are the most amazing creatures on the planet. She explained that ants use their jaws as they cut leaves. They take the leaves to their hills. They grow a special kind of food on the leaves.

Some kinds of ants make caves and nests deep under the ground. The ants can stay safe and keep their food there. They build in a special way so they won't drown while underground in the rain. You can read more about this on the next page.

People sometimes collect ants. They like to watch the ants march.

Student Model

DRAFT

Topic: How Ants Work and Live
Notes from "How Do Ants Live?"
Ants are the most amazing creatures on Earth.
ants' jaws cut leaves
Ants get leaves to take home.
They grow a special kind of food on the leaves.
Some kinds of ants make caves and nests deep under the ground.
The ants can stay safe and keep their food there.

Name where the information was found.

Jot notes. Not all notes must be in complete sentences.

Include only **information that tells more about your topic.**

Only facts, not opinions, should be included.

Use your **own words** to take notes.

---

1. Underline a sentence that does NOT belong in the notes because it tells an opinion.
2. Circle information that is NOT written in the student's own words.
3. Draw two lines under notes the student has jotted in phrases, not complete sentences.

Writer's Grammar
Place quotation marks around the title of an article.

Writer's Companion • UNIT 5
Lesson 1 *Topic and Notes*

LESSON 1: TOPIC AND NOTES

Name _____

Evaluating the Student Model

Evaluate Notes

How do you decide if someone has done a good job taking notes? Ask yourself these questions:

- Do the notes include only facts that tell more about the topic?
  (Read the topic. Then ask yourself what the notes explain about
  the topic. Think about whether the information states fact or opinion.)

- Does the writer use his or her own words?
  (Check the notes against where the information was found.)

A. Reread the Student Model on page 131. Then answer these questions.

   1. Write two sentences or phrases that seem to be in the student's own words.

   _____

   _____

   2. Why did the student not include information about ant collectors in the notes?

   _____

   _____

B. Evaluate the Student Model. Check the box next to each thing the writer has done well. Do not check the box if the writer did not do a good job with something.

- ☐ The notes tell where the information was found.
- ☐ Only information that tells more about the topic is included.
- ☐ The notes include facts, but not opinions.
- ☐ The notes are written in the student's own words.
- ☐ Some of the notes are jotted, but are still clear.

C. How do you think the writer could take more careful notes? Write your ideas on another sheet of paper.

Writer's Companion • UNIT 5
Lesson 1 *Topic and Notes*

See the rubric on page 207 for another way to evaluate the Student Model.

LESSON 1: TOPIC AND NOTES

Name _____

Revising the Student Model

Revise by Paraphrasing Information

What is one thing the student writer could have done better? The student could have paraphrased while taking notes. **Paraphrasing** means "writing in your own words." Here is an example of how a sentence from the Student Model could be improved.

Example They grow a special kind of food on the leaves.

They use leaves as a place to grow food.

A. Find two other sentences in the Student Model that are NOT written in the student's own words. First, write each sentence as the student wrote it. Then write the sentence in your own words.

1. Sentence from Student Model: _____

   _____

   A better way to write the notes: _____

   _____

2. Sentence from Student Model: _____

   _____

   A better way to write the notes: _____

   _____

B. On another sheet of paper, write the research topic you chose earlier. Begin your research by taking careful notes. Use as many sheets of paper as you need.

© Harcourt

Writer's Companion • UNIT 5
Lesson 1 *Topic and Notes*

LESSON 2: ORGANIZING INFORMATION

Name _____

Writer's Craft in Literature

Look at Organizing Information

What is the next step after you choose a topic and take notes? You organize your information. You write in a way that is interesting and makes sense. There are many ways to organize information. Here are three of the ways.

- Main idea and details: most important ideas with small pieces of important information to explain more about them
- Time order: events in the order they happened
- Compare and contrast: how things are alike and different

A. Read the following paragraph. Notice how the writer has organized information.

Literature Model

Roping was the most difficult skill for a cowboy to learn, and it was the most important. Cowboys carried ropes called lariats to lasso cattle. It took many months of practice to learn to spin the lariat and release it at just the right moment.

—from *Yippee-Yay!* by Gail Gibbons

B. Find the words that tell the main idea and details.
  1. Circle the main idea.
  2. Underline the sentences that tell important information about the main idea.

C. What kind of organization did the author use?

_____

Writer's Companion • UNIT 5
Lesson 2 *Organizing Information*

134

LESSON 2: ORGANIZING INFORMATION

Name _____

A Closer Look at Writer's Craft

Explore Organizing Information

Think about the information you will want to include in your research report. Then think about which kind of organization will work best for your report.

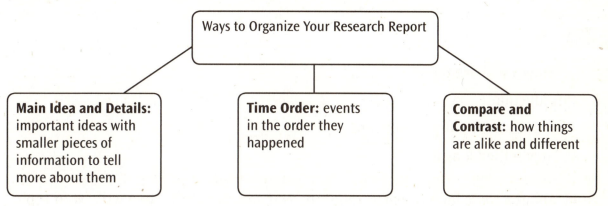

A. Read each paragraph. Circle the answer that tells how it is organized.

1.   Our library is filled with interesting books. They are grouped by type of book or subject. The library receives new books every month.

   a. main idea and details   b. time order   c. compare and contrast

2.   Fall and winter are alike in some ways. They are different in others. There are cold days during both seasons. Leaves change colors in fall. The trees are bare in winter, though.

   a. main idea and details   b. time order   c. compare and contrast

B. Read this paragraph from *Yippee-Yay!* Circle the answer that tells how it is organized.

   Next, the cowboys lassoed the calves. This was called chopping out. One by one, the calves were brought to a wood fire filled with heated branding irons. The cowboys took turns pressing a branding iron to each calf's hip, leaving a mark.

   a. main idea and details   b. time order   c. compare and contrast

C. Choose one of the kinds of organization. Circle it below. Then use it to write a short paragraph on another sheet of paper.

   a. main idea and details   b. time order   c. compare and contrast

Writer's Companion • UNIT 5
Lesson 2 *Organizing Information*

LESSON 2: ORGANIZING INFORMATION

Name _____

Practice with Writer's Craft

Use Organizing Information

Prepare to write an outline that organizes information for a research report. First, decide how you will organize your report. This student decided to organize her outline by main idea and details.

Example **My topic:** _The Anasazi community_____

    How I will organize: _main idea and details_____

  I. Introduction

     A. Anasazi were Native Americans.

     B. They settled long ago.

A. Think about a topic for a research report on Native Americans. Then write your topic. Tell how you will organize your report.

My topic: _____

How I will organize: _____

B. Research your topic. Take careful notes. Then write the first part of an outline for your research report.

  Title:

  I. Introduction

     A. _____

       _____

     B. _____

       _____

© Harcourt

Writer's Companion • UNIT 5
Lesson 2 *Organizing Information*

LESSON 2: ORGANIZING INFORMATION

Name _____

Focus on the Writing Form

The Parts of an Outline

An **outline** helps you organize ideas and information. Below is a draft of an outline written by a third grader. Look at the form of the outline. Note the information the writer included. Then answer the questions.

Student Model

DRAFT

**The Anasazi Community
by Keisha**

I. Introduction

    A. Anasazi were Native Americans.

    B. They settled long ago.

II. All the Anasazi helped with food.

    A. Men made things.

    B. Everyone farmed fields.

III. Home life was important.

    A. Men and women built homes.

    B. Women and children did things.

    C. Women and children made useful things.

IV. Conclusion

    A. The Anasazi became a strong community.

    B. They lived successfully for hundreds of years.

> **The introduction** tells the main idea of the report.

> Each main part of the outline includes a **Roman numeral followed by a period:** I. II. III. IV.

> The outline includes a **capital letter followed by a period** to show each important detail: A. B. C. D.

> In this outline, **the body (middle)** has facts organized under two main headings, II. and III.

> **Details** are organized in an order that makes sense.

> **The conclusion** restates and tells a bit more about the main idea from the introduction.

1. Draw an arrow to the topic of the outline.
2. Draw a box around the information in the introduction of the outline.
3. Circle the body of the outline.
4. Underline the conclusion in the outline.

Writer's Grammar
An outline has main topics and important details. Count how many topics are in this outline. Count how many important details there are.

© Harcourt

137

Writer's Companion • UNIT 5
Lesson 2 *Organizing Information*

LESSON 2: ORGANIZING INFORMATION

Name _____

Evaluating the Student Model

Evaluate an Outline

Ask yourself these questions to figure out whether an outline is strong:

- Does the writer include an introduction, a body, and a conclusion?
  (Look for the words *Introduction* and *Conclusion*. The body is the main part.)

- Does the writer include main parts and important details?
  (Look for Roman numerals and capital letters.)

A. Reread the Student Model on page 137. Then answer these questions.

    1. Think about the first paragraph that will come after the introduction. What will the paragraph be about?

_____

    2. What kind of organization did the writer choose? How can you tell?

_____

_____

B. Evaluate the Student Model. Check the box next to each thing the writer has done well. Do not check the box if you do not think the writer has done a good job.

- ☐ The writer included an introduction, body, and conclusion.
- ☐ The writer used Roman numerals to show main sections.
- ☐ The writer used capital letters before the important points.
- ☐ The details are organized in an order that makes sense.
- ☐ The conclusion restates and tells a bit more about the main idea of the report.

C. How do you think the writer could make the outline better? Write your ideas below. Use another sheet of paper if you need more space.

_____

_____

Writer's Companion • UNIT 5
Lesson 2 *Organizing Information*

138

See the rubric on page 207 for another way to evaluate the Student Model.

© Harcourt

LESSON 2: ORGANIZING INFORMATION

Name _____

Revising the Student Model

Revise by Adding Details

The student could have added more details to make the outline better. Here is an example of how part of the Student Model could be improved by adding more details.

Example **Original:**

   I. Introduction

      A. Anasazi were Native Americans.

      B. They settled long ago.

Revision:

   I. Introduction

      A. Anasazi were Native Americans.

      B. They settled in the Southwest more than 1,000 years ago.

      C. Everyone in the community had a special job.

A. Tell what you would do to revise the following part of the outline. You do not need to rewrite the outline. Just tell the kinds of things you would do to change it.

   II. All the Anasazi helped with food.

      A. Men made things.

      B. Everyone farmed fields.

_____

_____

_____

_____

B. Revise the beginning of the outline you wrote on page 136. Then complete the outline. Write your outline on another sheet of paper.

© Harcourt

Writer's Companion • UNIT 5
Lesson 2 *Organizing Information*

LESSON 3: WRITING A RESEARCH DRAFT

Name _____

Writer's Craft in Literature

Look at Writing a Research Draft

You have chosen a topic, taken careful notes, and made an outline. What is your next step? You will use your outline to write a draft of your research report. Your outline will guide you as you think about the introduction, middle, and end.

A. Read the following paragraph. Think about an outline the writer might have used to write the paragraph.

Literature Model

It took us twenty-one days on the stagecoach to get to California. When we got there, I thought we'd live with Pa in the gold fields. A whole tent city was built up. But Ma shook her head. "The gold fields are no place for children. We'll get a cabin and live in town."

—from *Boom Town* by Sonia Levitin

B. Identify details based on an outline.
1. Think about an outline the author might have created before writing the book. Circle the sentence that introduces the important idea.
2. Underline details that tell more about the important idea.

C. Write an outline you think the author might have used for this part of the book. Use another sheet of paper.

Writer's Companion • UNIT 5
Lesson 3 *Writing a Research Draft*
140

LESSON 3: WRITING A RESEARCH DRAFT

Name _____

A Closer Look at Writer's Craft

Explore Writing a Research Draft

Follow the order of ideas in your outline as you write your **research report draft.** The main parts of your outline, I., II., III., IV., will become the main parts and main ideas of your report. The details from your outline, A., B., C., D., will become the details in each main part.

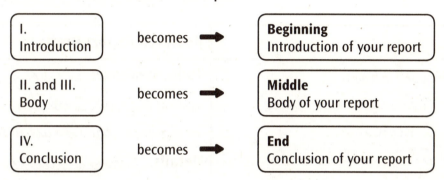

A. Read the parts of the outline. Tell what each part will become in the research report.

The Anasazi Community

I. Introduction
   A. Anasazi were Native Americans.
   B. They settled in the Southwest more than 1,000 years ago.
   C. Everyone in the community had a job.
II. All the Anasazi helped with food.
   A. Men hunted and made spears, bow, and arrows.
   B. Everyone farmed fields.
III. Home life was important.
   A. Men and women built homes.
   B. Women and children cared for households.
   C. Women and children made useful things.
IV. Conclusion
   A. The Anasazi became a strong community.
   B. They lived successfully for hundreds of years.

1. Part of the outline will become the beginning. Underline it.
2. Put a box around the part that will become the body.
3. Circle the part that will end the report.

B. Suppose you are ready to write about how the Anasazi will help with food. Which details from the outline will you put in your draft? Write them on another sheet of paper.

141

Writer's Companion • UNIT 5
Lesson 3 *Writing a Research Draft*

LESSON 3: WRITING A RESEARCH DRAFT

Name _____

Practice with Writer's Craft

Use Writing a Research Draft

Your outline will give you information to begin your research report. It will show you the main parts. It will also show you the details to include in each part. Here is how one third grader used an outline to begin a draft.

Example

Outline	Research Report Draft

I. Introduction
  A. Anasazi were Native Americans.
  B. They settled in the Southwest more than 1,000 years ago.
  C. Everyone in the community had a job.
	Topic Sentence: The Anasazi were Native Americans who settled in the Southwest.
	
	Details: They settled there more than 1,000 years ago. All the people in the Anasazi community had their own special jobs to do.

A. Look back to the outline you started in Lesson 2. Copy it below. Then complete the chart. Use the important points to write a topic sentence. Then add details.

Outline	Research Report Draft
	Topic Sentence: **Details:**

B. Use information from your chart to write a paragraph that supports your topic sentence. Use another sheet of paper.

Writer's Companion • UNIT 5
Lesson 3 *Writing a Research Draft*

142

© Harcourt

LESSON 3: WRITING A RESEARCH DRAFT

Name _____

Focus on the Writing Form

The Parts of a Draft

The main purpose of your **draft** is to present facts in a way the reader will understand. Your draft is not supposed to be a perfect piece of writing. There may be some errors in grammar or sentence order. Some important sentences may be left out. Here is part of a draft written by a third grader. Read to figure out if the writer has achieved the main purpose. Then answer the questions.

Student Model

The Anasazi Community
by Keisha

   The Anasazi were Native Americans who settled in the Southwest. All the people in the Anasazi community had their own special jobs to do.

   Home life to the Anasazi was very, very important. Men and women built their homes in the Cliffs on top of mesas. I wouldn't want to live up so high. The Anasazi settled in the Southwest more than 1,000 years ago. women and childern took care of the households. Women and children also made clothing, pots, and many other items.

- The report has a **title**.
- **The topic sentence** of the report tells the main idea of the whole report.
- **Each paragraph includes a topic sentence** to tell the main idea of the paragraph.
- The writer follows the **outline**.
- The writer includes **details and examples** from the outline.
- The report includes only **facts** about the topic.

1. Draw a box around the topic sentence of the whole report.
2. Circle the topic sentence of the second paragraph.
3. Underline the details in the second paragraph that support its topic sentence.
4. Compare the outline and the draft. Which sentence is out of order?

_____

_____

Writer's Grammar
Check to see that you have started each sentence with a capital letter. Find a sentence in the draft where the writer forgot to do this.

LESSON 3: WRITING A RESEARCH DRAFT

Name _____

Evaluating the Student Model

Evaluate a Draft

Ask yourself these questions to decide whether the draft is strong:

- Does the writer follow the points in the order in which they appear in the outline? (Compare the outline to the draft. Look for the specific main ideas and details.)

- Does each paragraph include a topic sentence with details to tell more about it? (Look for the topic sentence. Note the information in each detail.)

A. Reread the Student Model on page 143. Then answer these questions.

 1. Which detail sentence tells where the Anasazi built their homes?

 _____

 2. Which sentence does not belong in the second paragraph because it does not tell a fact?

 _____

B. Evaluate the draft by referring back to page 143. Check the box next to each task the writer has done well. Do not check the box if the writer has not done a good job.

 ☐ The writer used ideas from the outline.
 ☐ The writer followed the order of ideas from the outline.
 ☐ The writer included only facts about the topic.
 ☐ The writer wrote a topic sentence for each paragraph.
 ☐ The writer followed the outline to add facts and examples to support each topic sentence.

C. How do you think the writer could make the draft better? Write your ideas below.

 _____

 _____

 _____

Writer's Companion • UNIT 5
Lesson 3 *Writing a Research Draft*

144

See the rubric on page 207 for another way to evaluate the Student Model.

© Harcourt

LESSON 3: WRITING A RESEARCH DRAFT

Revising the Student Model

Name _____

Revise by Adding a Bibliography

The writer could have done a better job with the draft by including a bibliography. A bibliography lists the sources used for research. Each source is called an entry.

- The entries are written in alphabetical order based on the author's last name.

- Book titles are underlined or typed in *italics*.

Here is an example of how a bibliography entry can be improved. Note where the commas and periods have been placed in the revised entry.

Example **Book Entry**

Before Revision:	After Revision:
lopez, Rhonda, History of the Anasazi. New York: Fine Books, 2004	*Lopez, Rhonda. History of the Anasazi. New York: Fine Books, 2004.*

Author
Book title
Location and name of publisher
Date the book was published

A. Read the bibliography entries below. Revise each one. Make sure capitalization, punctuation, and form are correct.

1. *Neely, Pat. life in the Southwest. New York: Excellent Books, 2004.*

   Revised entry: _____

   _____

2. *ali, John, Native Americans of California. Chicago, Reigel, 2003.*

   Revised entry: _____

   _____

B. Return to the draft you began on page 142. On another sheet of paper, write two bibliography entries for resources you used.

© Harcourt

145

Writer's Companion • UNIT 5
Lesson 3 *Writing a Research Draft*

LESSON 4: REVIEW ORGANIZATION

Name _____

Writer's Craft in Literature

Review Organization

When you prepare to write a research report, you start by choosing a **topic.** Next, you take careful **notes.** You then use your notes to make an **outline.** The information in your outline will guide you in writing a **draft** of your report.

A. Read the paragraph. Notice how the writer has organized information.

Literature Model

Little pink cacao flowers grow right on the trunk. Green cacao pods grow side by side with the flowers, and next to them grow ripe yellow and red pods, ready to be picked. A cacao tree is always blooming, always ripening, and always ready to harvest.

—from *Cocoa Ice*
by Diana Appelbaum

B. Read the paragraph again. Think about how it is organized.

1. Underline the phrases that best help you figure out the topic of the paragraph.
2. Circle the kind of organization the writer uses in the paragraph.

    a. main idea and details   **b.** time order   **c.** compare and contrast

C. Write a phrase that tells the topic of the paragraph.

_____

_____

Writer's Companion • UNIT 5
Lesson 4 *Review Organization*

146

© Harcourt

LESSON 4: REVIEW ORGANIZATION

Name _____

A Closer Look at Writer's Craft

Review Organization

In this unit, you learned these steps to use when you organize.

1. Choose a **topic**. Be sure to narrow it for your writing.

2. Take **careful notes**. Write to tell where you find information. Write facts that tell more about your topic.

3. Use your notes to make an **outline**. Include main ideas and supporting details in an order that makes sense.

4. Use your outline to write a **draft** of your research report. Include the same main ideas and details. Your draft does not have to be perfect.

A. Look at the graphic organizer. Write the answers to the questions.

1. Why should you narrow your topic?

_____

_____

2. On what information are you taking notes?

_____

_____

B. Read these big ideas. Narrow each one to make a strong research report topic.

Example **Idea:** planets   **Topic:** _rings of Saturn_

1. **Idea:** weather   **Topic:** _____

2. **Idea:** cars   **Topic:** _____

3. **Idea:** birds   **Topic:** _____

147

Writer's Companion • UNIT 5
Lesson 4 *Review Organization*

LESSON 4: REVIEW ORGANIZATION

Name _____

Practice with Writer's Craft

Review Organization

Organization is important as you plan your report. The example in the box shows some of the notes a third grader wrote while planning a report.

Notes

Bees get their food from flowers.
Bees keep their food in the hive. They can eat it when it's too cold to fly to find more.
Young bees get their food from worker bees.
After bees find food, they do a kind of dance to show other bees where to go back to look for more.

A. Read the student's notes. Answer questions about the organization.

1. What big idea do you think the student writer had before choosing a topic? Why do you think so?

   _____

   _____

2. What topic do you think the writer chose when narrowing the big idea? Why do you think so?

   _____

   _____

B. Answer the question, based on the above outline.

What kind of organization do you think the writer will use: main idea and details, time order, or compare and contrast? Why do you think so?

_____

_____

_____

Writer's Companion • UNIT 5
Lesson 4 *Review Organization*

LESSON 4: REVIEW ORGANIZATION

Name _____

Focus on the Writing Form

The Parts of an Edited Research Report

You have learned how to choose a topic, take careful notes, make an outline, and write a first draft. After you write your draft, you will **edit** it. Here are some tips to help you as you edit.

EDITING TIPS	
REVISE	**PROOFREAD**
Make sure ideas are in an order that makes sense. Make sure all ideas are facts that tell more about the topic. Add words to connect ideas. Combine short, choppy sentences.	Indent paragraphs. Capitalize proper nouns. Make sure subjects and verbs agree. Check spelling and punctuation.

Here is a paragraph from a draft written by a third grader. Notice how the student made marks while revising and proofreading. Then answer the questions.

Student Model

DRAFT

The Anasazi Community by Keisha

Revised paragraph

Home life (to the Anasazi) was ~~very,~~ very important. Men and women built their homes in the Cliffs and on (top) of mesas. *the tops* ~~I wouldn't want to live up so high.~~ women and childern took care of the households. ~~Women and children~~ *They* also made clothing, pots, and many other items. *useful*

The Anasazi Community by Keisha

Proofread paragraph

Home life was very important to the Anasazi. Men and women built their homes in the Çliffs and on the tops of mesas. women and childern took care of the households. They also made clothing, pots, and many other useful items.

Use a separate sheet of paper to answer the questions. **Revised paragraph**
1. Which word was cut out of the first sentence?
2. Which sentence was cut out of the paragraph completely?
3. Which phrase in the paragraph was replaced with one word to make the sentences smoother and more interesting? What is the word that was put in place of the phrase?

Proofread paragraph
4. Which word was proofread to show it should be a capital letter?
5. In which word was a capital letter changed to lower case?

Writer's Grammar
When you proofread, put a slash through a capital letter to change it to a lower case letter. Find a slash in the Student Model.

149

Writer's Companion • UNIT 5
Lesson 4 *Review Organization*

LESSON 4: REVIEW ORGANIZATION

Name _____

Evaluating the Student Model

Evaluate an Edited Research Report

A. Two students were asked to edit a research report. This report received a score of 4. A score of 4 on a 4-point rubric means "excellent." Read the research report and the teacher comments that go with it. Find out why this research report is a success.

Student Model

DRAFT

The American Flag
by Betsy

The United States became a country in 1776. ~~There was~~ *and a new flag was needed for the new country.* ~~a new flag needed for the new country.~~ Some say that Betsy Ross made the first flag. They say that Betsy Ross was a clothing maker who made clothes for George Washington. ~~Betsy Ross had the same name as I do!~~

> Strong work! These sentences are better as a combined sentence.

> Glad to see you deleted this sentence. It did not tell an important fact about your topic.

There were thirteen colonies in 1776. The flag was made with one star for each of the thirteen colonies. It would be possible to sew on a new star for each *new* colony. The flag also had thirteen stripes of red and white. That would not change. It would always show how many colonies there were in the beginning.

> Nice job. You needed to add the word "new" to make this sentence clearer.

It is not known for sure if this story is true. it is known that the first flag had thirteen stars and thirteen stripes. It was a new flag for a new Country.

> Good proofreading. This is the first word of the sentence, so it should be capitalized.

> Good proofreading again. This is not a proper noun, so it should not be capitalized.

© Harcourt

Writer's Companion • UNIT 5
Lesson 4 *Review Organization*

150

LESSON 4: REVIEW ORGANIZATION

Name _____

Evaluating the Student Model

B. This paragraph got a score of 2. Why did it get a low score?

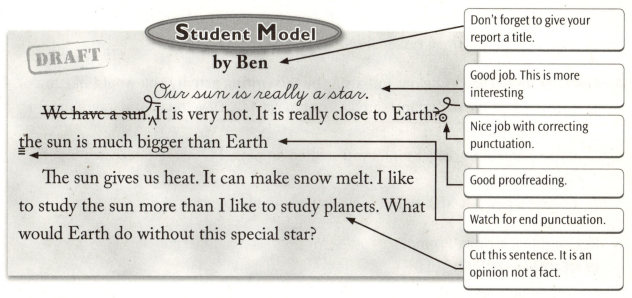

C. What score would you give the student's story? Put a number on each line.

	4	3	2	1
Purpose _____	☐ The topic is clear. The report includes only facts about the topic.	☐ The report topic is clear. The report includes mostly facts about the topic.	☐ The topic is somewhat clear. There is information that does not tell more about the topic.	☐ The topic and details are not clear. The report may contain opinions.
Organization _____	☐ The beginning, middle, and end are clear. Each paragraph has a topic sentence and supporting details.	☐ The beginning, middle, and end are not clear. Most paragraphs include a topic sentence and supporting details.	☐ The report does not have a beginning, middle, and end. Some paragraphs have details that support the topic.	☐ The report includes few details. Details in the report are not organized.
Grammar _____	☐ The writer uses correct grammar and punctuation.	☐ The writer makes a few mistakes in grammar and punctuation.	☐ The writer makes several mistakes in grammar and punctuation.	☐ The writer makes grammar or punctuation mistakes in almost all the sentences.

Writer's Companion • UNIT 5
Lesson 4 *Review Organization*

LESSON 4: REVIEW ORGANIZATION

Name _____

> **Extended Writing/Test Prep**

Extended Writing/Test Prep

On the last two pages of this lesson, you will use what you have learned
about organization to write a research report.

A. Read the three choices below. Put a star by the writing activity you would like to do.

1. Look back to the paragraph you wrote on page 142. Develop your paragraph into a complete report.

2. Choose one of the other topics you created on page 147. Write a research report about the topic.

3. Choose a new research report topic you would like to write about.

Respond to a Writing Prompt

REMEMBER—YOU SHOULD

- Decide on your topic.
- Take notes from sources about your topic.
- Organize your notes into an outline.
- Write a first draft and then revise it as you try to use correct spelling, capitalization, punctuation, grammar, and sentences.

USE THIS PREWRITING PAGE TO PLAN YOUR COMPOSITION.

B. Use at least three sources for research. Take careful notes. Make an outline. Then write your report. Begin your planning below.

TOPIC: _____

THE KIND OF ORGANIZATION I WILL USE: _____

_____

NAMES OF SOURCES AND NOTES I TOOK FROM EACH ONE: _____

_____

_____

_____

Use additional sheets of paper to take your notes.

Writer's Companion • UNIT 5
Lesson 4 *Review Organization*

LESSON 4: REVIEW ORGANIZATION

Name _____

Extended Writing/Test Prep

C. Create an outline on this page for your research report. Use the information from your notes. Be sure to use correct outline form.

D. Write your research report on other sheets of paper.

153

Writer's Companion • UNIT 5
Lesson 4 *Review Organization*

LESSON 5: WRITING TEST PRACTICE

Name _____

Writing Test Practice

Answering Multiple-Choice Questions

Some writing tests have questions with answer choices. This lesson will
help you practice this kind of test.

A. Some test questions may ask you about sentences. Read the test tip. Then shade the
bubble next to the correct answer for each question.

Read and answer questions 1–4.

1. In which sentence below is all **punctuation** correct?

   Ⓐ He bought carrots, and peas.

   Ⓑ He, bought carrots and peas.

   Ⓒ He bought carrots and peas.

2. In which sentence below is all **capitalization** correct?

   Ⓕ We traveled to another State to visit my Uncle.

   Ⓖ We traveled to another state to visit my uncle.

   Ⓗ We traveled to another State to visit my uncle.

> **Test Tip:**
> In question 2,
> only capitalize the
> words *uncle* and
> *aunt* if they come
> before a name.
> Example: Aunt
> Tam.

3. In which sentence below is all **punctuation** correct?

   Ⓐ I ran to the tree the lake and then home.

   Ⓑ I ran to the tree the lake, and then home.

   Ⓒ I ran to the tree, the lake, and then home.

4. In which sentence below is all **capitalization** correct?

   Ⓕ Her grandmother lives in Texas.

   Ⓖ Her grandmother lives in texas.

   Ⓗ Her Grandmother lives in Texas.

Writer's Companion • UNIT 5
Lesson 5 *Writing Test Practice*

154

© Harcourt

LESSON 5: WRITING TEST PRACTICE

Name _____

Writing Test Practice

B. Some test questions may ask you to read a passage and answer questions about it. The sentences in the passage may be numbered. Read the test tip.

DIRECTIONS

Read the passage below. Then read each question and fill in the correct answer on your Answer Sheet.

The Fair

(1) We likes to go to the fair. (2) We has gone many times. (3) Our fair is the best in the whole city. (4) We try to get there early. (5) We always stays in groups with friends and neighbors for safety.

1. What change, if any, should be made in sentence 1?
    A Change *We* to *Us*
    B Change *to* to *too*
    C Change *likes* to *like*
    D Make no change

2. What revision, if any, is needed in sentence 2?
    F We have gone many times.
    G We has goed many times.
    H We is going many times.
    J No revision is needed.

Test Tip: Find the action word in the sentence. This is the verb. Then figure out who is doing the action. This is the subject. Be sure the subject and verb agree.

3. What revision, if any, is needed in sentence 5?
    A We always stay in groups with friends, and neighbors for safety.
    B We always stay in groups with friends and neighbors for safety.
    C We always be staying in groups with friends and neighbors for safety.
    D No revision is needed.

Answer all test questions on this Answer Sheet.

1. Ⓐ Ⓑ Ⓒ Ⓓ   3. Ⓐ Ⓑ Ⓒ Ⓓ
2.   Ⓘ

155

Writer's Companion • UNIT 5
Lesson 5 *Writing Test Practice*

LESSON 5: WRITING TEST PRACTICE

Name _____

Writing Test Practice

C. Some test questions may ask you the best way to revise or correct sentences. Read the test tip.

Read the questions and answer them on the Answer Sheet.

1. Read this sentence.

   I want to _____ sure to _____ carrots for a tasty treat.

   Which pair of words makes the sentence correct?

   A   have, cutted

   B   be, cut

   C   was, cutted

   D   am, cut

> **Test Tip:**
> Some words are used to describe things. These words are called adjectives *(happy, old).*

2. Which sentence is written correctly?

   F   My cousins and Uncles are coming tomorrow for Thanksgiving.

   G   My cousins and uncles are coming tomorrow for Thanksgiving.

   H   My cousins and Uncles are coming tomorrow for thanksgiving.

   J   my cousins and uncles are coming tomorrow for Thanksgiving.

3. Which two words can describe something?

   A   bake, cake

   B   good, cake

   C   good, bad

   D   bake, bad

4. Which two words show action?

   F   bake, make

   G   good, cake

   H   bake, cake

   J   bake, bad

Answer all test questions on this Answer Sheet.								
1.	Ⓐ	Ⓑ	Ⓒ	Ⓓ	3.	Ⓐ	Ⓑ	Ⓒ Ⓓ
2.	Ⓕ	Ⓖ	Ⓗ	Ⓘ	4.	Ⓕ	Ⓖ	Ⓗ Ⓘ

Writer's Companion • UNIT 5
Lesson 5 *Writing Test Practice*

© Harcourt

LESSON 5: WRITING TEST PRACTICE

Name _____

Writing Test Practice

D. Some test questions may ask you about sentences in a paragraph. Read the test tip. Then read the passage and each question and mark the circle next to the correct answer.

Read *Party Day*. Choose the words that correctly complete questions 1–4.

Party Day

Today was party day at our ___(1)___. We got ready. We cleared away our books and papers. We ___(2)___ done this for parties before. Family members started to come. They brought juice and games. Nita's aunt came to help. I ___(3)___ my grandfather come in next. Today's party ___(4)___ better than our party last year.

1. Which answer should go in blank (1)?
   - (A) school's
   - (B) School
   - (C) school

2. Which answer should go in blank (2)?
   - (F) had
   - (G) was
   - (H) has

3. Which answer should go in blank (3)?
   - (A) see
   - (B) seen
   - (C) saw

4. Which answer should go in blank (4)?
   - (F) will be
   - (G) was
   - (H) is

Test Tip:
Remember that the name of a place is only capitalized when you are naming a specific place. In question 1, the name of the school is not given.

© Harcourt

157

Writer's Companion • UNIT 5
Lesson 5 *Writing Test Practice*

LESSON 1: IMAGERY AND FIGURATIVE LANGUAGE

Name _____

Writer's Craft in Literature

Look at Imagery and Figurative Language

Imagery is description that helps your readers make pictures in their minds. **Figurative language** is a kind of imagery. It can be used to compare one thing to another.

A. Read the Literature Model. Think about how the writer uses imagery in the stanzas of the poem.

Literature Model

You can tell
what's worth
a celebration
because
your heart will
POUND
and
you'll feel
like you're standing
on top of a mountain
and you'll
catch your breath
like you were
breathing
some new kind of air.

You know how
they come
from far away,
moving
up from the flats,
swirling
and swaying
and falling
and turning,
picking up sticks
and sand
and feather
and dry tumbleweeds.

—from *I'm in Charge of Celebrations*
by Byrd Baylor

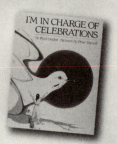

B. Identify imagery and figurative language.
   1. Circle examples of figurative language that compare.
   2. Underline examples of imagery that describe without comparing.

C. Read the figurative language in the poem. Which word helps you know that the writer is comparing? Write your answer. _____

Writer's Companion • UNIT 6
Lesson 1 *Imagery and Figurative Language*
158

LESSON 1: IMAGERY AND FIGURATIVE LANGUAGE

Name _____

A Closer Look at Writer's Craft

Explore Imagery and Figurative Language

Writers use sensory words to paint strong word pictures, or imagery.

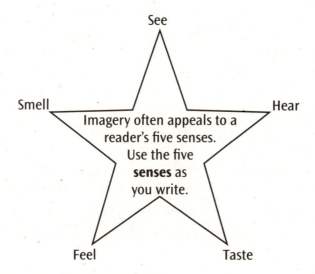

Imagery often appeals to a reader's five senses. Use the five **senses** as you write.

A. Read the sentences. Answer the questions to tell how the writer paints word pictures.

Example I touched the soft teddy bear.
Underline the word the writer uses to tell how the teddy bear feels.

I woke up and smelled sweet muffins baking. Then I raced outside and grabbed the icy, hard snow. Icicles hung from the roof like long, clear, pointed fingernails reaching to make snowballs.

1. Underline the word that tells how the muffins smelled.
2. Circle the words that tell how the snow felt.
3. Box the words that tell how the icicles looked.

B. Read this stanza from *I'm in Charge of Celebrations*. Underline the names of colors used to describe the cloud.

> It was not
> bluish-green
> or grayish-green
> or something else.
>
> This cloud
> was
> *green* . . .
> green as a jungle parrot.

C. Circle the line that shows the comparison used to describe the cloud.

Writer's Companion • UNIT 6
Lesson 1 *Imagery and Figurative Language*

LESSON 1: IMAGERY AND FIGURATIVE LANGUAGE

Name _____

Practice with Writer's Craft

Use Imagery and Figurative Language

Before you write an unrhymed poem, you may want to jot down some imagery to include. Here is how one third grader prepared to write a poem about summer. Notice that he chose to appeal to only two senses.

Example Title: _Summer Fun_

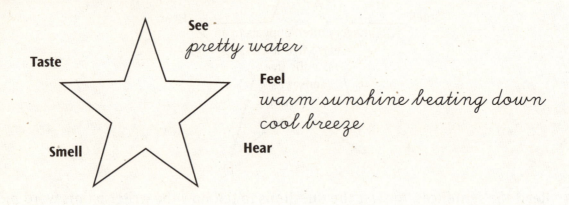

A. Prepare to write an unrhymed poem about a season or something you do outdoors. Write the title. Then fill in your star. Try to find some imagery for each sense, if possible.

Title: _____

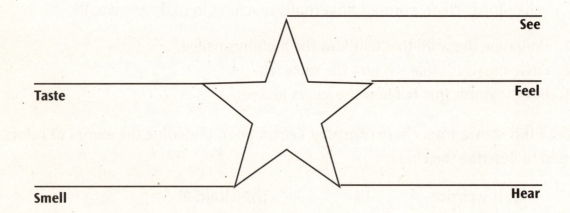

B. Use some of the senses from your star. Write the first stanza of your poem on another sheet of paper.

LESSON 1: IMAGERY AND FIGURATIVE LANGUAGE

Name _____

Focus on the Writing Form

The Parts of a Poem

A good **poem** guides readers to paint pictures in their minds. You can read a student's first draft of a poem below. Think about how the writer uses imagery to guide readers. Then answer the questions.

Student Model

DRAFT

Summer Fun
by Chase

The warm sunshine

beating down

feels so nice.

It follows me

to the pool

where I jump

into the pretty water.

The water feels like

a cool breeze.

Write a title for the poem.

Introduce the topic and write down the first image.

Add descriptive words and figurative language to describe the image.

Write about another image and repeat step two.

Check that the lines break in places that will help readers understand the poem.

1. Draw an arrow to the title of the poem.
2. Underline a word that describes the sunshine.
3. Circle the sentence that compares.
4. What does the writer describe first? _____
5. What does the writer describe next? _____

© Harcourt

Writer's Grammar
Poems are divided into stanzas. A line is usually skipped between stanzas. Count the number of stanzas in the Student Model.

161

Writer's Companion • UNIT 6
Lesson 1 *Imagery and Figurative Language*

LESSON 1: IMAGERY AND FIGURATIVE LANGUAGE

Name _____

Evaluating the Student Model

Evaluate a Poem

How do you decide if someone has done a good job writing a poem? Ask yourself these questions:

- Does the writer use strong, colorful words that clearly express ideas?
  (Look for sense words and words that paint strong pictures.)

- Does the poem make interesting comparisons?
  (Look for words such as *like* or *as*.)

A. Reread the Student Model on page 161. Then answer these questions.

1. Why does the writer describe the sun by saying that it *follows me?*

   _____

   _____

2. With what does the writer compare the water in the pool?

   _____

   _____

B. Now evaluate the Student Model. Put a check in the box next to each thing the writer did well. Do not check the box if you do not think the writer did a good job.

- ☐ The title and opening lines show the topic of the poem.
- ☐ The poem has images that show how the writer feels about the topic.
- ☐ The writer used strong, colorful words to describe the images.
- ☐ The poem makes interesting comparisons.
- ☐ The poem has sense words that paint pictures in the reader's mind.

C. How do you think the writer could make the poem better? Write your ideas on another sheet of paper.

Writer's Companion • UNIT 6
Lesson 1 *Imagery and Figurative Language*

See the rubric on page 207 for another way to evaluate the Student Model.

© Harcourt

LESSON 1: IMAGERY AND FIGURATIVE LANGUAGE

Revising the Student Model

Name _____

Revise by Creating a Strong Image

What is one thing the student writer could have done better? The writer
could have created stronger images. Here is an example of how a sentence
from the Student Model can be improved.

Example   The warm sunshine
beating down
feels so nice.

The warm sunshine
beating down
feels like a welcoming hug.

A. Revise these parts of the Student Model. Make the word pictures stronger. Add new
word pictures.

1. It follows me _____

to the pool _____

where I jump _____

into the pretty water. _____

2. Write a new sentence to add to the
first stanza. Create strong word pictures
with your sentence.

_____

_____

_____

_____

3. Write a new sentence to add to the
second stanza. Create strong word
pictures with your sentence.

_____

_____

_____

_____

B. Revise the stanza you wrote on page 160. Add figurative language and other imagery.
Use another sheet of paper.

© Harcourt

163

Writer's Companion • UNIT 6
Lesson 1 *Imagery and Figurative Language*

LESSON 2: VIVID VERBS

Name _____

Writer's Craft in Literature

Look at Vivid Verbs

Vivid verbs are action words that give strong, clear descriptions of what is happening. Vivid verbs help make language more colorful and interesting.

A. Read the following Literature Model. Think about how the writer uses vivid verbs.

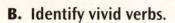

> A ground squirrel crept from the underbrush. Moving warily over the sand, it hesitated and looked around. Alejandro paused, keeping very quiet as the squirrel approached the garden. It ran up to one of the furrows, drank its fill of water, and scampered away. After it left, Alejandro realized that for those few moments his loneliness had been all but forgotten.
>
> —from *Alejandro's Gift* by Richard E. Albert

B. Identify vivid verbs.
  1. Underline the verbs in the passage.
  2. Circle vivid verbs that tell how the animals moved.

C. Write two vivid verbs that could replace *looked* in the paragraph.

_____

Writer's Companion • UNIT 6
Lesson 2 *Vivid Verbs*
164

LESSON 2: VIVID VERBS

Name _____

A Closer Look at Writer's Craft

Explore Vivid Verbs

Good writers use vivid verbs to make their writing interesting and clear. They form pictures in their own minds as they write.

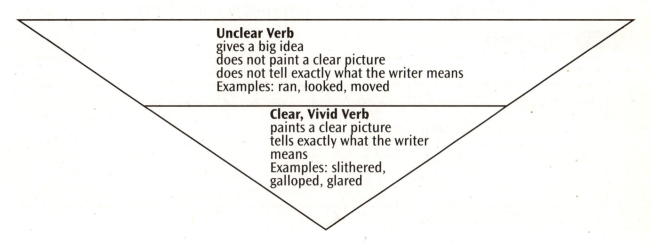

Unclear Verb
gives a big idea
does not paint a clear picture
does not tell exactly what the writer means
Examples: ran, looked, moved

Clear, Vivid Verb
paints a clear picture
tells exactly what the writer means
Examples: slithered, galloped, glared

A. Read each sentence. Rewrite the sentence by replacing the underlined verb with a vivid verb. If you wish, use verbs from the Word Bank.

Example He <u>asked</u> for just one more chance.

He begged for just one more chance.

1. The bear <u>went</u> away into the forest. _____
2. She <u>said</u> that she could do the job even better. _____
3. One puppy <u>took</u> the bone away from the other. _____

B. Read these sentences from *Alejandro's Gift*. Circle the one that gives a clearer description by using vivid verbs.

> The squirrel did come again, from time to time bringing along small friends.
>
> These were times he cherished, and he often stayed for hours, working until driven indoors by the desert heat.

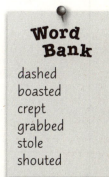

Word Bank
dashed
boasted
crept
grabbed
stole
shouted

C. Rewrite the sentence you did NOT circle above. Replace the unclear verbs with clear, vivid verbs. Use another sheet of paper.

165

Writer's Companion • UNIT 6
Lesson 2 *Vivid Verbs*

LESSON 2: VIVID VERBS

Name _____

Practice with Writer's Craft

Use Vivid Verbs

Prepare to write a thank-you letter. Think about why you are writing the letter and who will receive it. Will your verbs be clear and strong? Here is how one student made a list of vivid verbs while preparing to write a letter.

Example **Vivid Verbs**

Instead of *went*:	Instead of *fell*:
dashed, leaped, rushed, crawled, hopped, skipped, ran, drove	crashed, floated, tumbled

A. Think about verbs you plan to use in your letter. Write two of the verbs on the lines below. Then write vivid verbs to replace each one.

Vivid Verbs

Instead of _____:	Instead of _____:

B. Choose verbs from your chart that make your meaning strong and clear. Use them to write a thank-you letter for a gift or a favor. Use another sheet of paper for your writing.

Writer's Companion • UNIT 6
Lesson 2 *Vivid Verbs*

© Harcourt

LESSON 2: VIVID VERBS

Name _____

Focus on the Writing Form

The Parts of a Thank-You Letter

A good **thank-you letter** uses vivid verbs to explain why the writer is offering thanks. As you read the letter below, think about how the student writer uses vivid verbs. Then answer the questions.

Student Model

DRAFT

12 Maple Street
Orlando, Florida 32805
April 10, 20--

Dear Aunt Sophie,

Thank you so much for taking me camping. After we walked through the trees, I liked seeing the beautiful lake. The water bubbled over the rough rocks and went down the side of the cliff. I got a little bit scared when the tent flapped in the wind at night. You made me feel better, though. You said that everything would be okay. I hope we will be able to go back to the campground soon. Thank you again.

Love,
Riga

Write the address, date, and greeting.

Begin the body by stating what you are thanking the person for. Restate the thank you at the end.

Provide supporting examples. Include vivid verbs and specific nouns to add detail.

Conclude the letter.

Write the closing, and sign the letter.

1. Underline the heading.
2. Draw an arrow to the greeting.
3. Circle the body of the letter.
4. Write two vivid verbs from the letter. _____
5. Why are the vivid verbs important in the letter?

_____

Writer's Grammar
Place a comma after the closing in your letter. Write your signature on the line below the closing.

167

Writer's Companion • UNIT 6
Lesson 2 *Vivid Verbs*

© Harcourt

LESSON 2: VIVID VERBS

Name _____

Evaluating the Student Model

Evaluate a Thank-You Letter

When you evaluate a thank-you letter, ask yourself these questions:

- Does the letter include all the parts: heading, greeting, body, closing, and signature?
  (Look for the address and date, the *Dear* line, the paragraphs, and the signature below the closing.)

- Does the letter use vivid verbs and tell why she is thanking someone?
  (Look for verbs that are clear and strong.)

A. **Reread the Student Model on page 167. Then answer these questions.**

   1. Why is the student writing to thank her aunt?

   _____

   2. What vivid verbs helped you picture the camping trip?

   _____

B. **Now evaluate the Student Model. Put a check in the box next to each thing the writer did well. Do not check the box if you do not think the writer did a good job.**

- ☐ The letter has an address, date, and greeting.
- ☐ The letter includes a body that states what the writer is offering thanks for.
- ☐ The writer used many vivid verbs in supporting details.
- ☐ The letter includes a closing.
- ☐ The writer signed the letter.

C. **How do you think the writer could make the letter better? Write your ideas below.**

_____

_____

© Harcourt

Writer's Companion • UNIT 6
Lesson 2 *Vivid Verbs*

168

See the rubric on page 207 for another way to evaluate the Student Model.

LESSON 2: VIVID VERBS

Name _____

Revising the Student Model

Revise by Adding Vivid and Specific Words

What is one thing the student writer could have done better? The writer could have added more vivid verbs and other specific words. Here is an example of how a sentence from the Student Model can be improved.

Example The water bubbled over the rough rocks and went down the side of the cliff.

The water bubbled over the rough rocks and raced down the side of the cliff.

A. Revise these parts of the Student Model. Replace each underlined word to make it more vivid and clear.

1. After we <u>walked</u> through the trees,

   _____

2. I liked seeing the <u>beautiful</u> lake.

   _____

3. You <u>said</u> that everything would be okay.

   _____

B. Revise the thank-you letter you wrote on page 166. Add vivid verbs and other vivid, clear words. Finish your writing on another sheet of paper.

_____

_____

_____

_____

_____

_____

_____

© Harcourt

169

Writer's Companion • UNIT 6
Lesson 2 *Vivid Verbs*

LESSON 3: VIVID VERBS AND SPECIFIC NOUNS

Name _____

Writer's Craft in Literature

Look at Vivid Verbs and Specific Nouns

Good writers use **vivid verbs** and **specific nouns**. These action and naming words clearly show the writer's meaning.

A. Read the following Literature Model. Think about how the writer uses vivid verbs and specific nouns.

> ### Literature Model
>
> The answer is blowing in the wind. Day after day it whistles through the valley, picking up grit and sand and blasting everything it touches.
>
> The wind works like sandpaper, slowly wearing the rocks down and grinding them into weird and wonderful shapes.
>
> —from *Rocking and Rolling*
> by Philip Steele

B. Identify vivid verbs and specific nouns.
1. Underline the vivid verbs in the paragraph.
2. Circle the specific nouns in the paragraph.

C. Which word in the passage tells you how the wind sounds?

_____

Writer's Companion • UNIT 6
Lesson 3 *Vivid Verbs and Specific Nouns*

170

© Harcourt

LESSON 3: VIVID VERBS AND SPECIFIC NOUNS

Name _____

A Closer Look at Writer's Craft

Explore Vivid Verbs and Specific Nouns

Vivid verbs and **specific nouns** tell information in a clear and interesting way.

Vivid verbs paint clear pictures of action.

Using **vivid verbs and specific nouns** will tell your readers exactly what you want to say.

Specific nouns clearly tell your readers who, what, or where.

A. Read each sentence. Then rewrite the sentence by replacing the underlined noun with a specific noun.

Example Jesse played with his furry pet.

Jesse played with his furry dog.

1. Belinda scooped up the <u>vegetable</u>.

_____

2. Could you please hand me the <u>dish</u>?

_____

3. I could see the <u>feeling</u> in Grandpa's eyes.

_____

B. Read these sentences from *Rocking and Rolling*. Rewrite the second sentence to make the underlined noun clearer.

> Every year, there are 40,000 to 50,000 earthquakes that are strong enough to be felt. However, only about 40 of <u>them</u> are big enough to cause any damage.

_____

C. Now imagine that you are writing to tell how one of the 40 earthquakes would feel and look. Write two new sentences that include vivid verbs and specific nouns. Use another sheet of paper.

© Harcourt

Writer's Companion • UNIT 6
Lesson 3 *Vivid Verbs and Specific Nouns*

LESSON 3: VIVID VERBS AND SPECIFIC NOUNS

Name _____

Practice with Writer's Craft

Use Vivid Verbs and Specific Nouns

You are going to write a play about a problem. What will the problem be? What will your actors say? Write some verbs and nouns you plan to use. Then write new, clearer verbs and nouns that could replace unclear words. Here is how one student made lists of words to use.

Example

Unclear Words	Clear Words
Verb: falling	tumbling, pounding
Verb: open	start, flip
Noun: thing	doorstep, branch
Noun: clothes	sweater, coat, hat
Noun: place	house, room, door, floor

A. Read the unclear words that could tell about an emergency such as an earthquake or flood. Then write clear verbs and nouns to replace them.

Unclear Words	Clear Words
Verb: looked	
Verb: came	
Noun: animal	
Noun: colors	
Noun: people	

B. Choose some clear words from your chart. Use them to write the beginning of a play about an emergency such as an earthquake or flood. Do your writing on another sheet of paper.

Writer's Companion ▪ UNIT 6
Lesson 3 *Vivid Verbs and Specific Nouns*

172

© Harcourt

LESSON 3: VIVID VERBS AND SPECIFIC NOUNS

Name _____

Focus on the Writing Form

The Parts of a Play

A good **play** includes vivid verbs and specific nouns to introduce, develop, and solve a problem. Here is a third grader's draft of the beginning of a play. As you read, think about how the writer uses vivid verbs and specific nouns. Then answer the questions.

> ## Student Model
>
> **DRAFT**
>
> ### High Water
> ### by Clara
>
> (A family kitchen as heavy rain falls outside.)
>
> Oscar: Listen to the rain pound! Will it ever stop? Look outside. I can't even see the thing at the house across the street.
>
> Mom: I think we should get ready to leave.
>
> Grandmother: Let's flip on the TV first. The news can tell us how high the water is.
>
> Oscar: I tried. The TV won't work. I see water coming up to the top of the doorstep outside.
>
> Mom: Let's call the people for help.
>
> Grandmother: We can't. Our phone won't work.
>
> Oscar: We need to go to the safe place.
>
> Mom: Let's get the paper to figure out the best way to go.

Draft the beginning. Be sure to introduce the setting and characters.

Introduce the problem. Describe what problem or situation your characters are facing.

Develop the play. Write about the events that happen. Use details to make the events interesting to read. Remember to use the proper format for writing a play.

1. Draw an arrow to the title of the play.
2. Underline the information that tells where the play is happening.
3. Draw two lines under the words that tell which character is speaking.
4. Circle the vivid verb the grandmother uses to ask Oscar to turn on the TV.
5. What is the problem in the play?

Writer's Grammar
In a play, place a colon after the character's name before you write the words the character is saying.

173

Writer's Companion • UNIT 6
Lesson 3 *Vivid Verbs and Specific Nouns*

LESSON 3: VIVID VERBS AND SPECIFIC NOUNS

Name _____

Evaluating the Student Model

Evaluate a Play

When you evaluate a play, ask yourself these questions:

- Does the writer use vivid verbs?
  (Look for strong verbs that give a clear picture of the action.)

- Does the writer use specific nouns?
  (Look for clear nouns that tell you exactly what the writer means.)

A. Reread the Student Model on page 173. Then answer these questions.

1. One of the sentences in the play includes a vivid verb that tells how the rain sounds. Write the sentence below.

   _____

2. Which sentence includes a specific noun that helps you picture how deep the water is? Write the sentence below.

   _____

   _____

B. Now evaluate the Student Model. Put a check in the box next to each thing the writer did well. Do not check the box if you do not think the writer did a good job.

- ☐ The play has a title.
- ☐ The play tells where the action is happening.
- ☐ The characters' words include many vivid verbs and specific nouns.
- ☐ The writer introduced and developed a problem.
- ☐ The writer used the correct form to write the play.

C. How do you think the writer could make the play better? Write your ideas below.

_____

_____

Writer's Companion • UNIT 6
Lesson 3 *Vivid Verbs and Specific Nouns*

See the rubric on page 207 for another way to evaluate the Student Model.

© Harcourt

LESSON 3: VIVID VERBS AND SPECIFIC NOUNS

Name _____

Revising the Student Model

Revise by Adding More Vivid Verbs and Specific Nouns

What is one thing the student writer could have done better? The writer could have added more vivid verbs and specific nouns. Here is an example of how a sentence from the Student Model can be improved.

Example We need to go to the safe <u>place</u>.

We need to go to the safe shelter.

A. Revise these parts of the Student Model. Replace each underlined word to make it clearer and more specific. Use words from the Word Bank if you wish.

1. I can't even see the <u>thing</u> at the house across the street.

   _____

2. Let's call the <u>people</u> for help.

   _____

3. Let's get the <u>paper</u> to figure out the best way to go.

   _____

Word Bank

map
roof
newspaper
police
fence
neighbors
safe
shelter

B. Revise the beginning of the play you wrote on page 172. Add vivid verbs and specific nouns. If you need more space, use another sheet of paper.

_____

_____

_____

_____

_____

_____

© Harcourt

175

Writer's Companion • UNIT 6
Lesson 3 *Vivid Verbs and Specific Nouns*

LESSON 4: REVIEW WORD CHOICE

Name _____

Writer's Craft in Literature

Review Word Choice

Choosing words carefully can make your writing come alive. **Imagery** will help your readers "see" what you are writing about. **Figurative language** will paint a clear picture through comparing. **Vivid verbs** and **specific nouns** will tell your readers exactly what you mean.

A. Read the stanzas. Note how the writer has carefully chosen words.

Literature Model

> From space the earth was a big round ball,
> with swirling clouds of white
> against a deep-blue background,
> like the blue-black sky at night.
>
> Planets shone around them,
> reflecting starlike light.
> In that silent room floating in the dark,
> they traveled through the night.

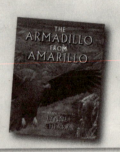

—from *The Armadillo from Amarillo*
by Lynne Cherry

B. Read the stanzas again. Find examples of figurative language and other imagery.
   1. Circle the figurative language that tells what the writer compares with the earth.
   2. Underline the example of imagery that tells where the characters are as they watch the scene.

C. Which phrases from the poem include color words that paint a clear picture for the reader?

_____

_____

LESSON 4: REVIEW WORD CHOICE

Name _____

A Closer Look at Writer's Craft

Review Word Choice

In this unit, you learned that careful word choices can make your writing clear and interesting.

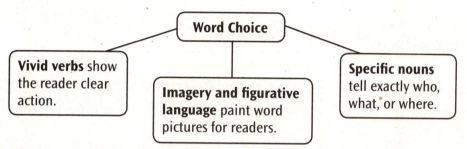

A. Read this paragraph. Think about how the writer carefully chooses words.

Snowflakes fell to the ground as quietly as cat paws touching the grass. Reina gazed through her frosty window. She slipped into her coat and pulled on her boots. Then she dashed out into the icy wonderland.

B. Write two examples from the paragraph for each of the following.

1. Figurative language _____
   _____

2. Vivid verbs _____
   _____

3. Specific nouns _____
   _____

C. Write two sentences you might add to the paragraph. Choose your words carefully. Include figurative language, vivid verbs, and specific nouns.

_____
_____
_____
_____

177

Writer's Companion • UNIT 6
Lesson 4 Review Word Choice

LESSON 4: REVIEW WORD CHOICE

Name _____

Practice with Writer's Craft

Review Word Choice

Before you write, you should think about making careful word choices.
Here is how one third grader made careful word choices while preparing
to write an invitation.

Example Kind of Invitation: _Surprise Party_

Nouns	Better, more specific nouns	Verbs	Better, more vivid verbs	Description	Better description, imagery
place thing person	park party Kia	comes say talk	appears shout cheer	no noise good food	as quiet as mice treats that will melt in your mouth

A. Use the chart to answer the following questions. Write your answers on the lines.

1. What other vivid verbs could you use for *comes* and *say*?

_____

2. What other imagery could you use for something that makes no noise?

_____

_____

3. What other imagery could you use for good food?

_____

_____

B. Write one to two opening sentences for an invitation to a surprise party.

_____

_____

_____

Writer's Companion • UNIT 6
Lesson 4 *Review Word Choice*

178

LESSON 4: REVIEW WORD CHOICE

Name _____

Focus on the Writing Form

The Parts of an Invitation

A good **invitation** might include imagery, vivid verbs, and specific nouns. Here is an invitation written by a third grader. As you read, think about how the student chose words carefully and organized the invitation. Then answer the questions.

Student Model

DRAFT

85 Greens Road
Kerrville, Georgia 30340
October 23, 20--

Dear Ms. Cherry,

Your book was like a bright light in our classroom. It was so amusing. On March 3, we will have authors come to our school at 85 Greens road in Kerrville, Georgia. We would be happy if you could come.

Authors will speak to students. Then we will serve cookies and juice. We will sing and dance in a show to give our thanks.

It would be a dream come true if you could come to visit our school on March 3 for Author's Day. Thank you.

Sincerely,
Rosario

> **Write a heading and greeting.** Write your address, the date, and a greeting for your invitation.

> **Draft the opening.** Introduce the topic of your invitation.

> **Develop the topic.** Include main ideas and details to describe the topic of your invitation.

> **Conclude.** Remember to include details about when and where the event will take place. Close and sign your letter.

1. Underline the heading of the invitation.
2. Circle the greeting.
3. Box two vivid verbs and two specific nouns.
4. Put [ ] around an example of figurative language.

Writer's Grammar
Remember to include the address in the heading of your invitation. What else is included in the heading?

Writer's Companion ▪ UNIT 6
Lesson 4 *Review Word Choice*

© Harcourt

LESSON 4: REVIEW WORD CHOICE

Name _____

Evaluating the Student Model

A. Two students were asked to write an invitation. This invitation received a score of 4. A score of 4 on a 4-point rubric means "excellent." Read the invitation and the teacher comments that go with it. Find out why this invitation is a success.

Student Model

DRAFT

62 Adams Street
Zane, Oregon 97402

February 10, 20—

Dear Officer Chin,

We are so glad that you watch out for the people in our town. Because you are so good at what you do, we would like for you to come and teach us more about safety. The Safety Fair will be at our school at 62 Adams Street on May 15. There will be people from all over the community coming to teach students about staying safe. We want to learn more about bike safety, walking home from school safely, keeping our homes safe, and many other things. Since we know that you are a walking encyclopedia when it comes to safety, we would love it if you could join us.

We will have many tables set up where students will visit to learn about safety. You can come to school early to have plenty of time to set up your table. We will have a lunch break at noon. There will be delicious sandwiches and the best fruit salad in town.

We would be really happy if you could come to our school on May 15 for the Safety Fair. Thank you.

Sincerely,

Clark

> Good job! You have included the correct heading.

> Yes! You have chosen words carefully to clearly tell about the event.

> Excellent use of figurative language.

> Nice work! You have developed the topic of the invitation.

> Good work with giving a reminder in the closing.

Writer's Companion • UNIT 6
Lesson 4 *Review Word Choice*

180

© Harcourt

LESSON 4: REVIEW WORD CHOICE

Name _____

Evaluating the Student Model

B. This paragraph got a score of 2. Why did it get a low score?

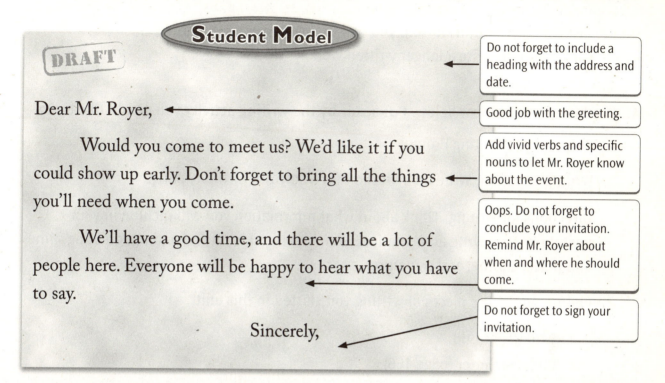

C. What score would you give the student's story? Put a number on each line.

	4	3	2	1
Form _____	☐ The writer includes a clear heading, greeting, body, closing, and signature.	☐ The writer includes at least four of the following: clear greeting, body, closing, and signature.	☐ The writer includes three or fewer of the following: greeting, body, closing, and signature.	☐ The writer's form is not clear.
Development _____	☐ The topic and time and place of the event are clear.	☐ The topic is clear, but time or place is not clear.	☐ The topic is clear; time and place are not clear.	☐ The topic, time, and place are not clear.
Word Choice _____	☐ The invitation is filled with imagery, vivid verbs, and specific nouns.	☐ The invitation includes some vivid verbs and specific nouns.	☐ The invitation includes very few vivid verbs and specific nouns.	☐ The invitation includes no vivid verbs or specific nouns.

181

Writer's Companion • UNIT 6
Lesson 4 Review Word Choice

LESSON 4: REVIEW WORD CHOICE

Name _____

> **Extended Writing/Test Prep**

Extended Writing/Test Prep

On the last two pages of this lesson, you will use what you have learned about word choice to write a longer written work.

A. Read the three choices below. Put a star by the writing activity you would like to do.

1. Respond to a Writing Prompt

   Writing Situation: Write an invitation for a surprise birthday party.

   Directions for Writing: Think about what information you will include in your invitation. Now write an invitation. Remember to include a heading, greeting, time and place, closing, and signature.

2. Choose one of the pieces of writing you started in this unit:

   - a poem (page 160)
   - a thank-you letter (page 166)
   - a play (page 172)

   Expand your beginning into a complete piece of writing. Use what you have learned about word choice.

3. Choose a topic you would like to write about. You may write a poem, a thank-you letter, or a play. Use imagery and figurative language, vivid verbs, and specific nouns.

B. Use the space below and on the next page to plan your writing.

TOPIC: _____

WRITING FORM: _____

HOW WILL I ORGANIZE MY WRITING: _____

_____

_____

_____

Writer's Companion • UNIT 6
Lesson 4 *Review Word Choice*

LESSON 4: REVIEW WORD CHOICE

Name _____

Extended Writing/Test Prep

C. In the space below, draw a graphic organizer that will help you plan your writing. Fill in the graphic organizer. Use the lines below to write notes and ideas for imagery, vivid verbs, and specific nouns.

Notes

_____

_____

_____

_____

_____

_____

_____

D. Do your writing on another sheet of paper.

183

Writer's Companion • UNIT 6
Lesson 4 *Review Word Choice*

LESSON 5: WRITING TEST PRACTICE

Name _____

Writing Test Practice

Answering Multiple-Choice Questions

Some writing tests have questions with answer choices. This lesson will help you practice this kind of test.

A. **Some test questions may ask you about sentences. Read the test tip. Then answer each question. Fill in the circle next to the best answer.**

Read and answer questions 1-4.

1. Which sentence is correct?
   - Ⓐ I'ts on the table near the bench where they're sitting.
   - Ⓑ It's on the table near the bench where they're sitting.
   - Ⓒ Its' on the table near the bench where the'yre sitting.

2. Which sentence is correct?
   - Ⓕ We taked our coats when it was time to go outside.
   - Ⓖ We took our coats when it was time to go outside.
   - Ⓗ We took our coats when it were time to go outside.

3. Which sentence is correct?
   - Ⓐ You're the one she's looking for right now.
   - Ⓑ Your the one shes' looking for right now.
   - Ⓒ Youre' the one she's looking for right now.

4. Which sentence is correct?
   - Ⓕ You was so happy when she helped you.
   - Ⓖ You were so happy when she help you.
   - Ⓗ You were so happy when she helped you.

> **Test Tip:**
> Remember that the apostrophe in a contraction usually goes in the place of the missing letter or letters.
> Example:
> he + is = he's

© Harcourt

Writer's Companion • UNIT 6
Lesson 5 *Writing Test Practice*

184

LESSON 5: WRITING TEST PRACTICE

Name _____

Writing Test Practice

B. Some test questions may ask you to read a passage and answer questions about it. The sentences in the passage may be numbered. Read the test tip, introduction, and the passage that follows. Then answer the questions on your Answer Sheet.

Maria is in the third grade. She wrote this story for her Language Arts class. She wants you to help her revise and edit the story. Read Maria's story and think about the changes she should make. Then answer the questions that follow.

Play at the Park

(1) She go to meet her friends when they're at the park. (2) They are all so happy to find out sh'es on the way. (3) They can't wait to see her. (4) Everyone plays on the slides and swings. (5) They have such a good time, and they say they will come again tomorrow.

1. What change, if any, should be made in sentence 1?
   A   Change *go* to **goes**
   B   Change *to* to **too**
   C   Change *they're* to **the'yre**
   D   Make no change

2. What is the BEST way to revise sentence 2?
   F   They are all so happy to find out shes' on the way.
   G   They be all so happy to find out she on the way.
   H   They are all so happy to find out she's on the way.
   J   No revision is needed.

3. What change, if any, should be made in sentence 3?
   A   Change *can't* to **cant**
   B   Change *wait* to **waits**
   C   Change *see* to **sees**
   D   Make no change

Test Tip:
Some verbs, such as *have*, *go*, and *take*, do not follow rules you have learned. You must learn the correct forms of these verbs by memory.

Answer all test questions on this Answer Sheet.

1. Ⓐ Ⓑ Ⓒ Ⓓ   3. Ⓐ Ⓑ Ⓒ Ⓓ

2. Ⓕ Ⓖ Ⓗ Ⓙ

Writer's Companion ■ UNIT 6
Lesson 5 *Writing Test Practice*

LESSON 5: WRITING TEST PRACTICE

Name _____

Writing Test Practice

C. **Some test questions may ask you the best way to revise or correct sentences in a paragraph. Read the test tip. Then answer each question. Fill in the circle next to your answer.**

The following is a rough draft of a student's paragraph. It may contain errors.

Feeling Better

(1) My sister have been home sick this week. (2) Her teacher asked me when she'd be comeing back to school. (3) I sayed that she was feeling better than she'd felt earlier in the week. (4) The teacher said she hoped my sister would get better quick. (5) I tooked my sister's books to her and put them in her room. (6) I think she'll be ready to do her homework soon.

> **Test Tip:**
> Ask yourself if the action in a sentence is happening now or if it happened in the past. This will help you choose the correct verb form.

1. Which underlined word is not used correctly?
   - Ⓐ My sister have been
   - Ⓑ teacher asked me how
   - Ⓒ better than she'd felt earlier
   - Ⓓ think she'll be ready

2. Which is the correct way to write sentence 2?
   - Ⓐ Her teacher asked me when shed be coming back to school.
   - Ⓑ Her teacher asked me when sh'ed be coming back to school.
   - Ⓒ Her teacher asked me when she'd be coming back to school.
   - Ⓓ Her teacher asked me when she'd be comeing back to school.

3. How should the underlined word in sentence 4 be correctly written?
   - Ⓐ quickly.
   - Ⓑ quickliest.
   - Ⓒ quickest.
   - Ⓓ Leave as is.

4. Which is the correct way to write sentence 5?
   - Ⓐ I taked my sister's books to her and put them in her room.
   - Ⓑ I took my sister's books to her and puts them in her room.
   - Ⓒ I tooked my sister's books to her and put them in her room.
   - Ⓓ I took my sister's books to her and put them in her room.

Writer's Companion ● UNIT 6
Lesson 5 *Writing Test Practice*

186

© Harcourt

LESSON 5: WRITING TEST PRACTICE

Name _____

Writing Test Practice

D. Some test questions may ask you to fill in sentences. Read the test tip. Then answer each question. Fill in the circle next to your answer.

Read "Camping." Choose the words that correctly complete questions 1–4.

Camping

We are a camping family! (1) _____ gone camping every summer since I was little. Last summer, we (2) _____ to a new campground. We could not drive very (3) _____ because it rained during the whole drive. We finally arrived at the campground. We waited in the car until the weather cleared. Then we (4) _____ our best to put the tent in the mud. We looked up to see a rainbow form. We will never forget that trip!

1. Which answer should go in blank (1)?
   - (A) Wev'e
   - (B) We've
   - (C) Weve

2. Which answer should go in blank (2)?
   - (F) go
   - (G) goes
   - (H) went

3. Which answer should go in blank (3)?
   - (A) fastly
   - (B) fast
   - (C) faster

4. Which answer should go in blank (4)?
   - (F) did
   - (G) done
   - (H) does

> **Test Tip:**
> Read carefully to see if a word describes a verb. If it does, it is an adverb. Be sure to choose the correct adverb form. In the sentence *The boy skated slowly*, the word *slowly* is an adverb.

© Harcourt

Writer's Companion • UNIT 6
Lesson 5 *Writing Test Practice*

Parts of Speech

The parts of speech are the different kinds of words you use in sentences.

Nouns are words that name people, places, or things.

> **Common nouns** name any person, place, or thing.
>> My **friend** moved here from a big **city.**

> **Proper nouns** name a special person, place, or thing.
>> **Oscar** moved here from **New York City.**

Verbs are action words that tell what people, places, and things do or are like.

> A verb's **tense** lets you know what time it is telling about.

> Verbs in the **present tense** tell about action that is happening now.
>> Oscar **pushes** his bike up the hill.

> Verbs in the **past tense** tell about action that has already happened.
>> Oscar **pushed** his bike up the hill yesterday.

> Verbs in the **future tense** tell about action that will happen later.
>> Oscar **will push** his bike up the hill tomorrow.

Pronouns are words that can take the place of nouns.

> A **subject pronoun** can take the place of a noun that is the subject of a sentence.
>> Oscar cared for the garden. **He** cared for the garden.

> An **object pronoun** can take the place of a noun that receives the action of a verb.
>> Oscar helped Mrs. Lin. Oscar helped **her** with the garden.

> A **possessive pronoun** takes the place of a noun that shows ownership.
>> Mrs. Lin's garden is filled with flowers. **Her** garden is beautiful.

Adjectives are words that tell about, or describe, nouns.

> **Cool** breezes blew across the **lovely** garden.

Articles are special adjectives. *A, an,* and *the* are articles. They come before nouns.

> Lin saw **an** ant on **the** top of **a** flower.

Writer's Companion
Writer's Grammar Guide

Writer's Grammar Guide

Prepositions are words that help a noun or pronoun join other words in the sentence.

We took the flowers **from** the garden. We gave them **to** a friend.

Conjunctions are joining words such as *and*, *but*, and *or*. Conjunctions take the reader from one thought to another.

Oscar gave seeds to Lin, **but** she grew her garden on her own.

© Harcourt

Writer's Companion
Writer's Grammar Guide

Sentences

A sentence is a group of words that tells a complete thought.

Complete sentences have a subject and a predicate. The subject is the naming part of the sentence. The predicate is the action part.

The sun shines.   The leaves and flowers grow on the plant.
SUBJECT PREDICATE   SUBJECT   PREDICATE

Fragments are groups of words that do not form complete sentences. Some fragments do not have subjects. Others do not have predicates.

FRAGMENT: Big drops of rain (Needs a predicate.)
FRAGMENT: falling from the sky (Needs a subject.)
COMPLETE: Big drops of rain are falling from the sky.

Run-on sentences are two or more sentences that run together into one sentence. They need to be divided into separate sentences.

RUN-ON: Flowers bloomed they were beautiful.
RUN-ON: Flowers bloomed, they were beautiful.
CORRECT: Flowers bloomed. They were beautiful.

Combining sentences can make writing more interesting and easier to read. Combine short, choppy sentences with a comma and words like *or*, *and*, *but*.

Oscar forgot to water the garden. Lin watered the plants for him.
Oscar forgot to water the garden, but Lin watered the plants for him.

Mrs. Lin grew flowers. Mrs. Lin grew vegetables.
Mrs. Lin grew flowers and vegetables.

© Harcourt

Writer's Companion
Writer's Grammar Guide

Capitalization

Some words must be capitalized. A word that is capitalized begins with a capital letter.

Capitalize the first word in a sentence.

> **We** drove to the lake.
> **The** weather was sunny.
> **All** of us were excited.

Capitalize proper nouns. These are words that name special people, places, or things.

> I saw my dad, my grandma, and my friend hop into the car.
> I saw **Dad, Grandma,** and **Ahmed** hop into the car.

> We couldn't wait to head for the lake.
> We couldn't wait to head for **Lake Gomez.**

Capitalize the street name in addresses.

> We stopped at 123 Maple Street for lunch on the way.

Capitalize the pronoun *I*.

> Ahmed and **I** sat in the back seat.
> He knew **I** would want to read and play games on the way.

Capitalize the first word, the last word, and all important words in a book title.

> I read part of *Harry Potter and the Goblet of Fire* during the drive.

Capitalize the title in a person's name.

> I read about **Doctor** Ruiz in one of my books.

© Harcourt

Writer's Companion
Writer's Grammar Guide

Writer's Grammar Guide

Punctuation

Punctuation marks are special marks used to make words and groups of words clear.

An end mark is used at the end of a sentence. It helps tell your reader what kind of sentence you are writing.

A **period** is used at the end mark of a **statement**. A statement tells something.

> We arrived at the lake in the early afternoon.
> Dark clouds filled the sky.

A **period** is used at the end of a **command**. A command tells someone to do something.

> Keep an eye on the sky.
> Watch for rain.

A **question mark** is used at end of a **question**. A question asks something.

> How long would we have to wait to swim?
> Would rain ruin our day?

An **exclamation mark** is used at the end of an **exclamation**. An exclamation shows strong feelings.

> The moon came out!
> Oh! It is beautiful!

Commas are used to separate words, parts of dates, or parts of sentences.

Commas are used after the **introductory words** in a sentence.

> **First,** we jumped in the water.
> **Yes,** I was the first one in the lake.

Commas are used to separate things in a list of three or more things.

> We put potato salad, sandwiches, and juice on the picnic table.

Commas are used in a greeting and a closing in a letter.

> Dear Ahmed,
> Sincerely,
> Pat

Commas are used to separate a month and date from a year.

> We went to the lake on August 5, 2006.

Writer's Companion
Writer's Grammar Guide

Writer's Grammar Guide

Commas are used to separate the name of a city from the name of a state.

> The lake is near Brownsville, Texas.

Apostrophes can be used to show ownership or to take the place of missing letters.

An **apostrophe** can show that someone has or owns something.

> family's lunch | parent's keys | Pat's book
> Grandma's car | Ahmed's game | bird's nest

An **apostrophe** can replace letters left out when a contraction is formed.

> is not | are not | we would | they are
> isn't | aren't | we'd | they're

> We aren't going to eat too much.   We'd like to swim again later.

Quotation marks are placed around the words someone says. The end mark usually goes inside the quotation marks.

> Ahmed said, "I'd like to go back in the water now."
> I asked, "How long until we have to leave?"

Abbreviations are shorter ways of writing words. An abbreviation usually begins with a capital letter and ends with a period.

WORD:	Friday	August	Mister	Doctor	Street
ABBREVIATION:	**Fri.**	**Aug.**	**Mr.**	**Dr.**	**St.**

© Harcourt

Writer's Companion
Writer's Grammar Guide

Usage

Usage tells people the correct way to speak and write.

Pural nouns are words that name more than one person, place, or thing.

Add -s to most nouns to form the plural.

SINGULAR:	horse	barn	farm	town
PLURAL:	horses	barns	farms	towns

Ten **horses** live in two **barns** on our **farms.**

Add -es to nouns that end in *s*, *ch*, *sh*, or *x*.

SINGULAR:	bus	bench	brush	fox
PLURAL:	buses	benches	brushes	foxes

We will wait on bench**es** for the bus**es** to go visit the farm.

Change the *y* to *i* and add –*es* if a noun ends in *y*.

SINGULAR:	city	pony	puppy	penny
PLURAL:	cities	ponies	puppies	pennies

I saw ten pon**ies** and four pupp**ies.**

Possessive nouns show that someone has or owns something.

Add 's to a singular noun to form the possessive.

SINGULAR:	pony	friend	dog
PLURAL:	pony's	friend's	dog's

The pony**'s** food was near the dog**'s** bone.

Add only an apostrophe (') to a plural noun that ends in *s*.

SINGULAR:	ponies	friends	dogs
PLURAL:	ponies'	friends'	dogs'

Some of my friends' books had pictures of ponies' barns.

Contractions are formed by putting two words together. Use an apostrophe to replace letters left out when a contraction is formed.

TWO WORDS:	is not	are not	we would	they are	will not
CONTRACTION:	isn't	aren't	we'd	they're	won't

Writer's Companion
Writer's Grammar Guide

Writer's Grammar Guide

Subject-Verb Agreement The verb in a sentence must agree with the subject.

A **singular subject** must have a **singular verb.** You usually add *-s* to the verb for the singular form.

> The **girl likes** to visit the farm.

A **plural subject** must have a **plural verb.** Do not add *-s* to the verb for the plural form.

> The **girls like** to visit the farm.

Adjectives and Adverbs can be used to compare people, places, things, and actions.

Compare with the correct form of an adjective.

Add *-er* to most adjectives to compare two people, places, or things.

> The horse is tall**er** than the pig.

Add *-est* to most adjectives to compare three or more people, places, or things.

> The horse is the tall**est** of all the farm animals.

Describe and compare with the correct adjective: *good, better, best.*

Use *good* to describe one person, place, or thing.

> Visiting the farm was a **good** field trip.

Use *better* to compare two people, places, or things.

> Visiting the farm was a **better** field trip than visiting the zoo.

Use *best* to compare three or more people, places, or things.

> Visiting the farm was the **best** field trip all year.

Compare with the correct form of an adverb.

Add *-er* to most adverbs to compare two actions.

> The pony ran fast**er** than the dog.

Add *-est* to most adverbs to compare three or more actions.

> The pony ran fast**est** of all.

Tell about most verbs with the adverb *well*, NOT with the adjective *good.*

> The bus driver drove **well** on the field trip to the farm.

© Harcourt

Writer's Companion
Writer's Grammar Guide

Writer's Grammar Guide

Double Negatives

Negatives are words such as *no, not, nothing,* and *never.*

Use only one of these words in a sentence.

> WRONG: The hens **never** laid **no** eggs.
> CORRECT: The hens **never** laid eggs.
> ALSO CORRECT: The hens laid **no** eggs.

> WRONG: Do**n't never** forget to feed the chicks.
> CORRECT: Do**n't** forget to feed the chicks.
> ALSO CORRECT: Do**n't ever** forget to feed the chicks.

> WRONG: He doesn**'t** like to clean **no** barns.
> CORRECT: He doesn**'t** like to clean barns.
> ALSO CORRECT: He doesn**'t** like to clean **any** barns.

> WRONG: The farmer did **not** do **nothing** last week.
> CORRECT: The farmer did **nothing** last week.
> ALSO CORRECT: The farmer did **not** do **anything** last week.

Irregular verbs have different forms than most verbs.

The verb *be*

PRESENT: *am, is, are*

> I **am** on the farm now.   You **are** on the farm now.   She **is** on the farm now.

PAST: *was, were*

> I **was** there earlier.   You **were** there earlier.   She **was** there earlier.

The verb *go*

PRESENT: *go, goes*

> I **go** to the barn today.   He **goes** to the barn today.

PAST: *went*

> I **went** to the barn yesterday.   He **went** to the barn yesterday.

The verb *do*

PRESENT: *do, does*

> I **do** chores today.   She **does** chores today.

PAST: *did*

> I **did** chores yesterday.   She **did** chores yesterday.

Writer's Companion
Writer's Grammar Guide

Writer's Grammar Guide

Tricky Words

There are some tricky words to learn about.

Homophones are words that sound the same but have different spellings and meanings.

to, too, two

Word	Meaning	Sentence
to	toward	I am going **to** the store.
too	more than enough; also	My dad is going, **too.** **Too** many people are shopping.
two	the number 2	We'll come back in **two** hours.

there, their, they're

Word	Meaning	Sentence
there	at that place	I can't wait to get **there.**
their	belonging to them	Many people are getting in **their** cars.
they're	they are	I'm glad **they're** leaving.

its, it's

Word	Meaning	Sentence
its	belonging to it	My dog needs a new tag for **its** collar.
it's	it is	**It's** time to pay for the collar and go home.

Watch for other homophones such as: *ant/aunt, ate/eight, eye/I, be/bee, blew/blue, cent/sent, hear/here, hi/high, hole/whole, know/no, meat/meet, pair/pear, read/red, right/write, road/rode, sea/see, son/sun, threw/through, weak/week, who's/whose, wood/would, your/you're.*

© Harcourt

Writer's Companion
Writer's Grammar Guide

Homographs are words that are spelled the same but have different meanings.

can

Meaning	Sentence
able to	I **can** put the new tag on the collar.
container	Then I'll open a **can** of dog food.

bit

Meaning	Sentence
took a bite of	My dog **bit** into the food.
small piece	My dog only ate a little **bit**.

Spelling Tips

These tips will help you spell many of the words you use.

Short Vowel Sound

The short vowel sound is usually spelled with one vowel.

a: bat fast   *e:* let when   *i:* with little   *o:* drop job   *u:* cut funny

Long Vowel Sound

The long vowel sound is sometimes spelled **vowel + consonant + e.**

make shape   **wide** smile   **joke** tone   **tune** flute

Soft *c* and hard *c*

The letter *c* can stand for the **hard *c* sound** or the **soft *c* sound.**

hard *c:* car cold cave   soft *c:* cent face ice

The letter *c* is usually followed by *i, e,* or *y* if a word has the soft *c* sound.

place, rice, race, pencil, center, dance

Soft g and hard g

The letter *g* can stand for the **hard *g* sound** or the **soft *g* sound.**

hard *g:* go gate   soft *g:* gym giant

Writer's Companion
Writer's Grammar Guide

Writer's Grammar Guide

The letter **g** is usually followed by *i, e,* or *y* if a word has the soft *g* sound.

> cage, gentle, giraffe, huge, page, stage

Silent Letters

Silent *k* You need to remember which words begin with silent *k*.

> knee knife knew knight knock

Silent *w* You need to remember which words begin with silent *w*.

> wrap wreck write wrong wrote

Adding *–ed* or *–ing* to a word that ends in *e*

If a word ends in *e*, drop the *e* before you add *–ed* or *–ing*.

> like liked   nap napping   bake baking

Spelling Words to Practice

These words can be hard to spell. Practice spelling them until you know them well.

about	address	again	all right	already	always	because	busy	could
enough	friend	once	people	receive	sure	together	tonight	trouble

© Harcourt

Writer's Companion
Writer's Grammar Guide

Conventions

Proofreading Strategies

Our language follows **conventions,** or rules. We write in sentences. We end them with punctuation marks. We leave spaces between words, and we indent paragraphs. All of these conventions help readers understand what we write.

As you proofread your writing, you should check to make sure you have followed the conventions. These strategies will help you proofread:

Wait before proofreading.

Put your writing away for a while. Then come back to it. You may see new things.

Proofread in steps.

1. Look at your **sentences.** Are they complete? Are they written correctly? Are your **paragraphs** indented?
2. Check your **language use.** Do your subjects agree with your verbs? Have you used the correct forms of adjectives and adverbs? Have you followed the rules for **capitalization** and **punctuation?**
3. Last, check your **spelling.** Circle any words that look strange. Use a dictionary if necessary.

Proofread with a partner.

Two pairs of eyes are better than one. Your classmate may find mistakes you did not see.

Writer's Companion
Proofreading Strategies

Proofreading Checklist

This checklist will help you as you proofread your work.

Sentences and Paragraphs

☑ Is every sentence complete?

☑ Does each sentence begin with a capital letter and end with the correct end mark?

☑ Is each paragraph indented?

Grammar and Usage

☑ Do your verbs agree with their subjects?

☑ Have you used the correct verb tenses?

☑ Have you used *I* and *me* correctly?

☑ Have you used the correct form of adjectives and adverbs that compare?

Capitalization and Punctuation

☑ Have you capitalized proper nouns and the pronoun *I*?

☑ Have you used commas, quotation marks, and apostrophes correctly?

Spelling

☑ Are you sure of the spelling of every word?

☑ Have you always used *there* and *their* correctly?

☑ Have you spelled plural nouns correctly?

Symbol	Meaning
	delete text
	insert text
	move text
	new paragraph
	capitalize
/	lowercase
	correct spelling

Technology

If you use a computer spell checker, remember that it cannot tell homophones apart. For example, the spell checker does not know whether you mean *here* or *hear*.

Presentation

Presenting Your Work

Sometimes you write for yourself. Most of the time, you write for other people. When you let other people read or hear your writing, you **publish** your work.

You can publish your writing in many ways. Here are some ideas.

Publishing Ideas for Any Type of Writing

- Read your writing aloud.
- Have a friend read it silently.
- Post it on a bulletin board.

Publishing Ideas for Descriptions and Poems

- Draw or paint a picture to go with your writing.
- Cut pictures from a magazine. Make a collage.
- Make up a dance to go with your writing.
- Find a piece of music to go with your writing. Make a tape recording in which you read while the music plays in the background.

Strategies Good Writers Use

- Use your best handwriting.
- Add drawings that help your readers understand and enjoy your writing.

© Harcourt

Writer's Companion
Presenting Your Work

202

Presentation

Publishing Ideas for Stories

- Work with friends. Act out your story.
- Draw pictures to go with your story.
- Read your story aloud to another class.
- Make a class storybook.
- Send your story to a magazine.
- Mail your story to a relative far away.

Acting Out a Story

You can follow these steps to perform a story or a personal narrative.

Step 1

Plan how the people in your story should sound to the audience. What are their voices like? How do they say their words? Experiment with your voice.

Step 2

Find props for your story. You can use different kinds of clothing, pictures, and other items.

Step 3

Decide how you want to present your story. Do you want to read it just as it is written, or do you want act it out? You could even ask classmates to help you present your story as a play.

Technology

You can use the computer to make a neat copy of your work. Type the words the way you wrote them. Use **Return** and then **Tab** to start a new paragraph.

Writer's Companion
Presenting Your Work

Presentation

Publishing Ideas for Reports

- Add maps and pictures. Make a tabletop display.
- Make a poster for the classroom bulletin board.
- Teach your classmates about your topic.
- Put your report in the classroom library for others to read.

Publishing Ideas for Persuasive Writing

- Send a letter to the editor of your school paper.
- Give a speech to your class.
- Publish your ideas on your school's website.
- Read your work aloud. Take a poll. Find out who agrees with you.

Strategies Good Writers Use

- Give your work a title.
- Put your name on your work.
- Check your facts and proofread carefully before you send a letter in the mail or post work on a website.

Writer's Companion
Presenting Your Work

Presentation

Giving an Oral Report

Strategies	Applying the Strategies
Make note cards.	• Write each main idea on a note card. Put your cards in order, and number them.
Practice.	• Give your talk to a friend or family member. Think about how to make your talk better.
Speak clearly and slowly.	• Speak more slowly than you do when you're just talking. Look at your audience. Remember that they can learn from you.

Strategies for Listeners

- Think about the speaker's main idea.

- Try to learn from what you hear.

- Ask questions to learn more.

© Harcourt

Writer's Companion
Presenting Your Work

Writer's Glossary of Terms

adjective: a word that describes a **noun**

adverb: a word that describes a **verb,** an **adjective,** or another **adverb**

compare and contrast essay: an essay that tells how things are alike and different

descriptive paragraph: a **paragraph** that tells what something or someone is like

detail: a fact, event, or statement; details usually tell about a main idea

dialogue: words spoken by characters in a story or play

directions: writing that tells how to do something

essay: a piece of writing that is not a story, usually with a clear purpose for writing

fact: something that is true

how-to essay: an **essay** that tells how to do something

letter: a written message to someone

letter of invitation: a letter asking someone to come to an event

main idea: what something is mostly about

notes: writing that records facts or ideas from a source of information

outline: a system for organizing information and notes

paragraph: a group of sentences with a single main idea or topic

paragraph of information: a paragraph that presents facts and data

paragraph of explanation: a paragraph that tells how something works or what something is like

paragraph that compares: a paragraph that tells how things are alike

paragraph that contrasts: a paragraph that tells how things are different

paragraph that explains: a paragraph that tells how something is done, what something is like, or how to do something

personal narrative: a story about the experiences of the writer

personal story: a story about what happened to the person who wrote the story

persuasive paragraph: a paragraph that tries to convince someone to do something or to think a certain way

play: a story written for the stage

poem: a piece of writing, often with rhyme

predicate: what the subject of a sentence does or is like

purpose for writing: the reason why someone writes something

reason: why something happens or is true

research report: a piece of writing that comes from study and from looking things up

review: a piece of writing that sums up and gives an opinion about a story, book, play, or movie

rubric: a guide for scoring or evaluating something

sensory detail: a detail that "speaks" to one of the senses—sight, sound, touch, smell, or taste

sequence: the order in which things happen

speech: a spoken message or statement

story: a made-up tale

subject: what a sentence is about

summary: a short piece of writing that wraps up the main points of a longer piece of writing

thank-you letter: a letter telling someone you liked and appreciated something they gave or did for you

topic: what something is about

verb: a word that names an action

Writer's Companion
Writer's Glossary of Terms

Scoring Rubric for Writing

	Score of 4	Score of 3	Score of 2	Score of 1
	☆☆☆	☆☆☆	☆☆	☆
FOCUS/IDEAS	The paper is completely focused on the task and has a clear purpose.	The paper is generally focused on the task and the purpose.	The paper is somewhat focused on the task and purpose.	The paper does not have a clear focus or a purpose.
ORGANIZATION/PARAGRAPHS	The paper has a clear beginning, middle, and ending. The ideas and details are presented in logical order. The writer uses transitions such as *Finally, The next day,* or *However,* to show the relationships among ideas.	The ideas and details are mostly presented in logical order. The writer uses some transitions to show the relationships among ideas.	The organization is not clear in some places.	The paper has little or no organization.
DEVELOPMENT	The paper has a clear central idea that is supported by strong specific details.	The paper has a central idea and is supported by details.	The paper does not have a clear central idea and has few supporting details.	The central idea is not clear and there are few or no supporting details.
VOICE	The writer's viewpoint is clear. The writer uses creative and original phrases and expressions where appropriate.	The writer's viewpoint is somewhat clear. The writer uses some original phrases and expressions.	The writer's viewpoint is unclear.	The writer seems uninterested in what he or she is writing about.
WORD CHOICE	The writer uses clear, exact words and phrases. The writer uses creative and original phrases and expressions where appropriate.	The word choices are clear. The writer uses some interesting words and phrases.	The writer does not use words or phrases that make the writing clear to the reader.	The writer uses word choices that are unclear or inappropriate.
SENTENCES	The writer uses a variety of sentences. The writing flows smoothly.	The writer uses some variety in sentences.	The writer does not use much variety in his or her sentences.	There is little or no variety in sentences. Some of the sentences are unclear.
CONVENTIONS	There are few or no errors in grammar, punctuation, capitalization, and spelling.	There are a few errors in grammar, punctuation, capitalization, and spelling.	There are some errors in grammar, punctuation, capitalization, and spelling.	There are many errors in grammar, punctuation, capitalization, and spelling.

207

Writer's Companion
Student Rubrics

Scoring Rubric For Writing

	Score of 6	Score of 5	Score of 4	Score of 3	Score of 2	Score of 1
	★★★★★★	★★★★★	★★★★	★★★	★★	★
FOCUS	The writing is completely focused on the topic and has a clear purpose.	The writing is focused on the topic and purpose.	The writing is generally focused on the topic and purpose.	The writing is somewhat focused on the topic and purpose.	The writing is related to the topic but does not have a clear focus.	The writing is not focused on the topic and purpose.
ORGANIZATION	The ideas in the paper are well-organized and presented in logical order. The paper seems complete to the reader.	The organization of the paper is mostly clear. The paper seems complete.	The organization is mostly clear, but the paper may seem unfinished.	The paper is somewhat organized, but seems unfinished.	There is little organization to the paper.	There is no organization to the paper.
SUPPORT	The writing has strong, specific details. The word choices are clear and fresh.	The writing has strong, specific details and clear word choices.	The writing has supporting details and some variety in word choice.	The writing has few supporting details. It needs more variety in word choice.	The writing uses few supporting details and very little variety in word choice.	There are few or no supporting details. The word choices are unclear.
CONVENTIONS	The writer uses a variety of sentences. There are few or no errors in grammar, spelling, punctuation, and capitalization.	The writer uses a variety of sentences. There are few errors in grammar, spelling, punctuation, and capitalization.	The writer uses some variety in sentences. There are a few errors in grammar, spelling, punctuation, and capitalization.	The writer uses simple sentences. There are some errors in grammar, spelling, punctuation, and capitalization.	The writer uses simple sentences. There are many errors in grammar, spelling, punctuation, and capitalization.	The writer uses unclear sentences. There are many errors in grammar, spelling, punctuation, and capitalization.

Writer's Companion
Student Rubrics

© Harcourt